W9-CLQ-092

THE KAPSIKI OF
THE MANDARA HILLS

THE KAPSIKI OF
THE MANDARA HILLS

Walter E.A. van Beek

State University of Utrecht, The Netherlands

WAVELAND
PRESS, INC.
Prospect Heights, Illinois

For information about this book, write or call:

Waveland Press, Inc.
P.O. Box 400
Prospect Heights, Illinois 60070
(708) 634-0081

Copyright © 1987 by Waveland Press, Inc.

ISBN 0-88133-284-4

All rights reserved. No part of this book may be reproduced, stored in a retrieval system, or transmitted in any form or by any means without permission in writing from the publisher.

Printed in the United States of America

7 6 5 4 3 2

Contents

Preface

Within Cameroon and Nigeria, the Mandara hills represent one of the last areas of Central and Western Africa to be modernized. Exploration and colonization started much earlier elsewhere. Still, the Mandara hills have been on the fringe of hectic political and military developments throughout the centuries, thus subjecting the inhabitants to varied pressures. The Kapsiki of Cameroon and the Higi of Nigeria are two tribes from this region; they are part of a dense scattering of a few larger and many smaller tribal units populating the inaccessible hillsides. Although quite similar to one another, the assorted tribes are sufficiently different to warrant specific description. The Kapsiki and the Higi form one coherent group of villages, although they are usually considered as two separate ethnic units. When necessary, we shall use both names: Kapsiki and Higi. Normally, we shall use the term Kapsiki for both.

Research in the Mandara hills has been intensive in the last decade. Our research among the Kapsiki/Higi has been underway since January 1971. From March 1972 through August 1973 we lived in the village of Mogodé, in the approximate center of the Kapsiki region. Even though our presentation in the following chapters relates explicitly to that village, Mogodé is fairly representative of Kapsiki villages in Cameroon and Nigeria. Follow-up visits in 1979 and 1984 complemented our data and graduate students researched specific topics from 1983 through 1985. The project has been made possible by the Netherlands Foundation for the Advancement of Tropical Research (grant W52-91) and the State University of Utrecht, Holland.

No research project is done single-handedly. I gratefully acknowledge the help of my colleagues who reviewed the manuscript, Stephen Pern for his linguistic reviewing, and George Spindler for his general advice. Mrs. Kootje Willemse and Mrs. Hetty Nguema Asangono typed the manuscript. My deepest gratitude goes to the two parties most involved in my work—my family and the many dear Kapsiki friends whose friendship made the research an unforgettable experience.

W.E.A. van Beek
Utrecht, The Netherlands

Figure 1: Map of the Kapsiki/Higi Area

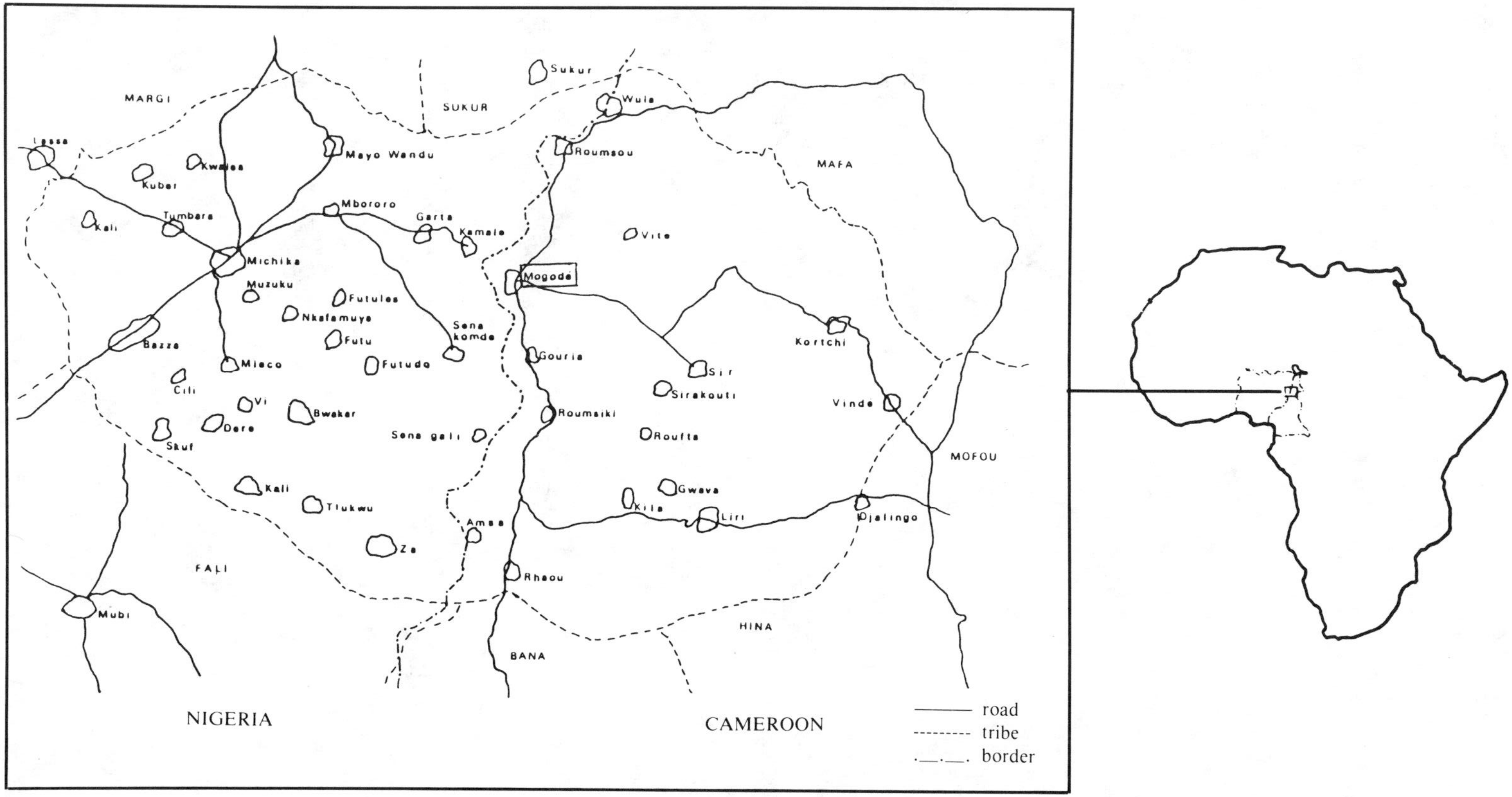

road ——————
tribe - - - - - -
border —·—·—·—

MAFA

MOFOU

Kortchi

Vinde

Djelingo

Sir
Sirakouti
Vite

Roufta

Gwava

Liri
Kila

HINA

Wula

Roumsou

Sukur

SUKUR

Mogode

Gourla

Roumsiki

Rhoumzou

Rhaou

BANA

CAMEROON

Mayo Wandu

Mbororo
Garta
Kamale

Sena Komde

Ama

Kwabes

Tumbere

Michika

Muzuku
Futules

Ndafamuye
Fulu

Futudo

Sena gali

Za

Kubel

Kali

Bazza

Mieca

Vi
Dere

Cili

Sauf

Bwaker

Kali

Tiuku

FALI

NIGERIA

Lassa

Mubi

CAMEROON

ix

Pronunciation of Kapsiki Words

a = last
e = the
E = yet (represented in text by *E)*
i = his
u = through
ɗ = implosive d (represented in text by *ɗ*)
g = good
j = jealous
r = palatal
rh = gutteral
t| = |:bilateral fricative
c = church

1

The Fight

Mogodé, February 1953

The village of Mogodé is at war with Sirakouti. Some twenty-five men from each village face each other yelling, running, dodging enemy arrows while shooting their own, and throwing spears. Two men with buffalo-hide shields team up with an archer using the two shields as a cover for all three. Slowly and cautiously they steal forward over the open battleground. Within shooting distance they part the shields and the archer lets fly at the nearest enemy. The Sirakouti man dodges the poisoned arrow; he throws his javelin at the threesome. He, too, misses. Along the battle line individual warriors try other ruses to catch their adversaries unaware. A daring young warrior, anxious to prove himself, takes a run to the front, pretending to aim at a particular Sirakouti. He turns quickly to hit another enemy and then zigzags back behind the skirmish line. At the south end of the battleground a group of Sirakouti men suddenly withdraw, tempting their adversaries to pursue them. The Mogodé recognize the well-known stratagem of a fake retreat and do not take the bait. Seeing that the trick does not work, a group of fresh soldiers emerges from the Sirakouti rear.

Most of the fighting and shooting is between individuals. The men select their place in the line and spend most of their fighting time trying to hit their direct opponent. Opposing warriors with some type of close relationship avoid each other: no man should shoot at a kinsman, in-laws or ritual allies. The fight knows no leader. Every man tries to stand out in battle in order to gain a reputation as a real fighter—someone who runs fast and who shoots quickly and well. Experienced warriors avoid risks more than the young

1

boys who just passed initiation this year; the elders try to keep the boys from overly reckless fighting. Experienced fighters are well-known among friend and ally. The enemy knows them too and concentrates on targeting at the most famous. Killing or capturing such an adversary is concrete proof of fighting ability. Only a minority of the people present are actually fighting. The majority watch the proceedings from the background. The tired warriors rest a while and old men reminisce about their battles. The scene is dominated by women. Almost all the women of the village are present; they yell and scream, exhorting the men to greater exploits, scolding those who are holding back, and weeping for the wounds of the warriors. With baskets filled with arrows and cowhorns full of poison, some blacksmiths remain in the background helping the fighters to poison their arrow heads. Children swarm over the battle area and the boys often are used to pick up enemy arrows. This is a dangerous job but men fear killing children, even those of the enemy. As the Kapsiki say, "whoever kills an uninitiated boy will not see his own son go through initiation."

The fighting between Mogodé and Sirakouti that has started before noon continues till sunset without any casualties. The arrows have found no victims yet, although two people have been wounded by spears. The barbed heads make ugly wounds when removed, but the wounds will heal. In the late afternoon a Sirakouti man is wounded by an arrow. His kinsmen flock around him, yelling and wailing. The poison may mean a quick death. A clan brother pulls the arrow back as far as the barbed head allows and with his knife carves out all the flesh pulled up by the arrow. If the wounded man should die with the arrow in his body, it is believed that all his clansmen will fall under the arrows. Therefore, the lethal object is cut out even if death may result from the operation. Boys and women run to the village to boil water and the Sirakouti man is transported to his compound. Once there, a blacksmith washes him with the steaming hot water and tamarind leaves to sweat the poison out. A grilled chicken is fed to him in order to see whether he can chew the bones. When the women see that he does not have the strength to do so, they wail and lament as if he is dead already. The blacksmiths start preparations for burial.

This death puts an end to fighting for that day. While Sirakouti people are busy with the burial (a man slain in battle is buried the next day, in contrast to the normal burial which takes three days), the direct kinsmen occupy themselves with plans for revenge. The following day they will be the fiercest fighters on the battlefield, trying to make the other village pay for this death. It does not matter whether the actual killer of their brother is slain, a death for a death is the important thing. The enemy, knowing that retaliation is due, will be very careful in preparation for the coming fight. Early next morning each man will consult his blacksmith diviner and sacrifice according to his instructions. He will confess any breaches of taboo and will take his most powerful protective medicine into the field.

Two ritual functionaries will perform protective rites. The village priest will slaughter a chicken, and the hunting leader will gather the men behind his compound, shooting an arrow in the direction of the enemy village and sprinkling dust over the men before sending them to the battlefield.

But all this will come tomorrow. Today's fighting is over. Most men have already forgotten what the fight was about and many of them never knew. What started it in the first place? The dispute was over a woman. As is common in Kapsikiland, the fight started between two men who had married the same woman. In this case the woman from Mogodé called Kwava had grown tired of Sunu, the Mogodé spouse she had married as a girl, six years before. Selling fritters at the market of Sirakouti, she met Deli, who appeared to be wealthy. He made her a nice present of a piece of mutton for dinner. This week she went to that market again and arranged for her lover to take her to his compound. Sunu, her Mogodé husband, noticed his wife's absence that evening and immediately suspected she had left him. A neighbor told him he had seen her walking east, so Sirakouti market had obviously been her goal.

It was pitch-dark when Sunu cautiously sneaked between the compounds of Sirakouti, creeping toward the one of his *kwesegwe,* his mother's brother. This relative told him where his errant wife was and helped him find the way. Arriving at the compound of Deli, Sunu was confronted with a new problem. All Kapsiki compounds consist of a number of huts enclosed by a man-high stone wall, a fortress to the casual observer. The only entrance is guarded by two stone pillars some two meters high which lead to the main resting and gathering place and several huts. It is, therefore, impossible to enter without arousing the residents. Furthermore, Deli had a dog which would likely be guarding the entrance. So Sunu circled the huge compound wall in stealthy reconnaissance. Hearing Kwava's voice, he went over to that part of the wall and softly called her name. On the north side the compound wall had deteriorated and Sunu climbed into his enemy's home. His wife duly offered no resistance, but on their way out his *zamale* (new husband of his wife) overtook him. Sunu was forced out of the compound through the exit where Deli's friends and neighbors had quickly gathered after hearing the yells of both men. Deli was furious and only let Sunu go after beating him black and blue. Of course he did not let Kwava go. Sunu staggered back home, enraged and insulted. As the woman's first husband, he should not have been beaten up—his rights to her were strong enough to guarantee immunity—and he was justifiably indignant at being treated like a *zakwatewume* (husband of a run-away woman).

Back in Mogodé he explained his plight to some clan brothers living near him. They were livid, informed the other men and prepared for fighting. The next morning when people from other villages arrived at the Mogodé market, the Mogodé men grabbed some innocent Sirakoutians, clubbed them and chased them home. After that, war was imminent. The Sirakoutians armed themselves and so did the people of Mogodé. Both parties ran screaming and yelling to the battleground at the frontier between the two villages.

This conflict took place in 1953. Up to that time, battles between neighboring villages were common, as were conflicts with outside enemies (other tribes). Since 1953 almost no battles have been fought. This old incident, however, is important in understanding the Kapsiki way of life. War has had a deep influence on Kapsiki society; we shall focus on that in Chapter Three. Even more important is the setting of the war and the reason it was fought. Present-day Kapsiki life cannot be understood without reference to fighting. The lay-out of the villages, internal organization, and the values adhered to by the people are all products of the warlike past. Changes in the region must be assessed with this past in mind. Finally, the very same structures and processes that developed as a response to insecurity are still operative today. The main theme of this book, how marriage functions in a system with an exceptionally high divorce rate, serves as a prime example. Marital relationships are heavily influenced by the hostility between villages which still lingers on today, by the fabric of kinship groups that make up a village and by the deeply rooted values about how men and women should behave, feel and think.

The main themes of Kapsiki society are present in the opening battle. Autonomous villages make up the backbone of Kapsiki territorial organization. No authority exists on a tribal level; even within the village authority is spurious. Kapsiki are individualists. Compared to other African tribes, they are far less inclined to communal living and action than most of their compatriots. In this respect a Kapsiki shows quite a few "western" features and values. His home is his castle, and he eagerly defends his autonomy and privacy against neighbors, kin and community. Thus, socially, Kapsiki society is fragmented compared to other African tribes in which communal action, village interests and authority usually are stronger. This fragmentation may be a result of the isolation of the area as well as the wars and slave raids of its past. It is a feature the Kapsiki share with most other tribes of the Mandara mountains.

Of the few groups which extend beyond the village border, the blacksmiths are the most important. We encountered blacksmiths in battle, serving as a munition depot, but staying out of the fray themselves. They would never engage in actual fighting, as they have kinsmen all over the area, in every village. They form a sort of caste in Kapsiki society; they have their own specific work (smithing, burial, music and divination) and are strictly endogamous: they only marry among themselves. Their social position in the village is definitely lower than the "normal" Kapsiki, although they are richer and better fed. At the end of Chapter Two the special position of the blacksmith will be described.

Within the village, kinship groups bind individuals together; patrilineal clans and lineages are the most important. In Chapter Three we will occupy ourselves with this kinship aspect. Kinship ties through the mother (matrilateral relations) also have a role to play inside as well as outside the village.

In the chapter on religion (Chapter Four), it will be shown how this social system, with its inherent problems and tensions, finds its expression in religion. How individual men and women cope with social and marital situations and how people manipulate the system in which they live are best illustrated by their belief in and reactions toward the supernatural world.

Kapsiki marriage is a very brittle institution. The great majority of women sooner or later leave their husbands in search of new (and presumably better) spouses. The men continually try to bind their women to them or to persuade other women to join them in marriage. Polygamy, technically polygyny (one man having plural wives) is an essential feature of the system. All this will be described in detail in Chapter Five, which forms the core of the book.

In Chapter Six we shall summarize the major trends in Kapsiki social and marital life and try some modest assessment of the way in which Kapsiki culture enhances the changes for survival of its members. Chapter Seven outlines some expectations for the future of Kapsiki society.

In a brief description such as this, no systematic comparison with other African tribes is possible. At the end of each chapter, and occasionally throughout the text, we will make some comparisons between the Kapsiki situation and that of other African peoples. The purpose of these comparisons will be to place the Kapsiki into some perspective as to their specific cultural features.

2

Coping with Mountains and Men

This chapter deals with the general historical, geographical and ecological background of the Kapsiki society. As has been argued previously, some knowledge of the past is essential for understanding the present. The general picture that emerges is one of an isolated area in which a relatively poor people defended themselves against enemies with superior weaponry and organization. The Mandara mountains made such a defense possible.

The mountain area offered more than a retreat from slave raiders or hostile neighbors. Its relatively fertile soils and dependable rainfall facilitated a horticultural economy based on sorghum and millet cultivation, with some cattle and goat husbandry. In this economy, a fixed division of labor between the sexes can be shown which is an important factor in the relationship between men and women.

A crucial role is played by the blacksmiths whose technology makes Kapsiki agriculture possible. At the same time, blacksmiths perform many functions which sustain social, as well as economic, life. We will explore their position in Kapsiki society and their specific functions as a means of discovering the important themes running through Kapsiki culture. The blacksmith culture serves as a counterpoint to mainstream Kapsiki society.

Slavery

The Mandara Mountains where the Kapsiki live have long served as a slave reserve for the Moslem empires of the Sudan. Among these, the empire of Kanem-Bornu (Urvoy 1949), the sultanate of Mandara (Vossart

6

1952) and the Fulani Sokoto empire (Kirk-Greene & Hogbin 1969) are the most important. Slave raids in the Mandara area figure prominently in the first information available about Kanem-Bornu enterprises (Urvoy 1949). When the Mandaras living at the northern end of the Mandara range were Islamized in the sixteenth century, they eagerly participated in raiding the so-called Kirdi (heathen) mountain populations. At the start of the eighteenth century the Mandara were subjugated by Bornu, and through the two following centuries the sultans of Mandara paid approximately one hundred slaves a year as a tribute to Bornu (Le Moigne 1918:132). In the eighteenth century the Fulani, originally a nomadic people devoted to their cattle, burst out in holy war *(jihad)* subjugating almost all of Northern Nigeria and Northern Cameroon (Kirk Greene & Hogbin 1969). The difference for the Kirdi was only slight. It simply meant a different enemy and the usual threat. The basic relationship remained the same since they were still a hunting area for slaves. This was the situation encountered by the first European to arrive. The first contact of European explorers with the mountain tribes took place during a slave raid. In 1823 Major Denham, travelling from Bornu to the Niger, reported how a Kirdi tribe gave two hundred slaves to the sultan of Mandara in order to avoid a raid (Denham 1826:313). According to his estimate, about a thousand slaves a year were captured in the Mandara mountains and sold in the markets of Mora, the capital of the Mandara sultanate. Friends of the sultan could expect the gift of a Kirdi village to raid and plunder. As far as Denham's escort was concerned:

> The Arabs were all eagerness; they eyed the *Kirdy* huts, which were now visible on the sides of the mountains before us, with longing eyes, and contrasting their ragged and almost naked state with the appearance of the sultan of Mandara's people in their silk robes, not only thought but said: "If Boo-Khaloom (their leader) pleased, they would go no further; this would do" . . . Boo-Khaloom was, as usual, very sanguine; he said he would make the sultan handsome presents and that he was sure a town full of people would be given to him to plunder (Denham 1826:197).

Barth, another famous explorer of Africa's interior, reported a Bornu slave raid on the mountains of the Mandara in 1852 in which 500 slaves were captured (Barth 1857:195). Of course the Kirdi did not succumb to these raids without striking a blow. In fact, they fought the Muslim cavalry fiercely whenever it penetrated the mountains. The steeper the hillsides, the more successful was the defense. In the southern part of the Mandara region, where slopes are gentle and the hills are low, the Kirdi had a very hard time. The Goudé and Njeign tribes, who now inhabit this countryside, were eventually subdued and Islamized. Up north, where steep rocky slopes dominate the scene, no mounted invader ever succeeded in subjugating Kirdi tribes like the Kapsiki, Matakam, Goudour and Mofu. As the small plateau which forms the center of the Kapsiki territory is a suitable battleground for horses, the Kapsiki withdrew to the volcanic outcroppings that are dispersed over the undulating plain; they also built earth ramparts in the narrow valleys surrounding this plateau as a defense against surprise raids. Although the enemy had superior weaponry, this bow-and-arrow defense against a mounted adversary could be effective. The Fulani met some bloody defeats, and around 1600 one of the most famous emirs of Bornu fell during a slave raid in the Mandara regions.

Despite this spirited defense the pressure must have been great. Slaves were captured in considerable numbers, raids could be expected at any time and in any place. As a result the Mandara Kirdi developed a high resistance to outside influences. They resisted Islam as the religion of their enemies. On the other hand, none of the tribes ever developed a centralized political authority. The Kirdi tribes never became strong homogeneous units; authority hardly ever transcended village or "massif" level (1). A quick look at an ethnic map clearly shows this. This small mountain area harbors more than 30 different ethnic units. Most of them do not exceed 10,000 members, but a few, like the Kapsiki, number more than 100,000. The internal organization of each unit remains fragmented. No structural innovations took place to cope with the Muslim threat, no military organizations, no centralized decision-making procedures, no organization of guards nor any multi-village alliances were ever made. A few villages might group their forces for an occasional fight, but after the battle cooperation ended.

Slave raids from outside were never an isolated phenomenon. Villages also fought each other, as our opening chapter illustrated. One of the two aims of these internal battles was capturing slaves (killing enemies was the other); hence, the use of non-lethal weapons like spears and clubs. Any enemy — man, woman or child — could be taken. A child might be adopted by the family of the captor, a woman could be married, but a captured man did not stay in the village. He became a slave who was either sold back to his original village or sold to Fulani or Hausa merchants. The price was much higher from the merchants and might amount to a bull, twenty goats or sheep and one or more gandouras (wide Fulani gowns). This happened only when his kinsmen could not (or would not) furnish a ransom of, for example, one cow and ten goats. The merchants sold slaves in the market of Sokoto, Yola or some other distant town. Travel was exceedingly difficult for runaway slaves; therefore, few succeeded in returning to their native villages. The Kirdi in the Mandara mountains also owned slaves from distant areas:

> Mbriki, in Mogodé, is a slave no longer. He was raised in Bornu, cap-
> tured at the age of eighteen, and sold into the Mandara area. His owner
> provided him with a place to build his compound and with a wife to
> raise children. Mbriki cultivated the fields of his owner, for the benefit
> of both his owner and himself. He is a member of his owner's clan, in a
> father-son relation.

A slave was not readily distinguished from a free man in daily life. His owner (buyer) gave him a plot to build a house, furnished a brideprice to marry a woman and in all respects acted as his social father. His lower status was revealed only on a few occasions: in disputes and conflicts his owner acted on his behalf and there were some rituals and festivals from which he was excluded. At the *rhena za* (men's talk) he was not expected to speak but remained seated in the background, applauding softly with the blacksmiths when his owner or his kinsmen were addressing the listening crowd. When his daughters married, the brideprices were collected by his owner. In the wet season he had to cultivate some fields on behalf of his owner before tending the fields he had received from his "father." He was a member of his owner's clan and lineage as well as the owner's mother's clan. His children were not slaves.

Captured women were simply married by their captors; the main difference with other women was that no brideprice was paid. Among the women in the compound such a wife might have a low status and her children might be derided as children of a slave, but this was not an important difference. If she was very prolific, her status was enhanced. After the pacification by the Europeans slaves were freed. Since most of them had built their homes and raised their families among their owner's people, most did not leave. Some, however, returned to their home country:

> Hamadou, an Islamized Kapsiki, was captured as a slave in a war between Mogodé and Gouria at the age of twenty. His kinsmen were too poor to pay a ransom; thus, he was sold through Fulani merchants to Kanem. After the pacification he returned to Mogodé, an old man. Having lived so long in Kanem country he had to relearn how to be a Kapsiki—language, customs, etc.

The Kirdi in the Mandara mountains remained marginal to the great Muslim empires of the Sudan. From the southward expansion of Kanem in the twelfth century resulting in the empire of Bornu, to military domination by the Fulani in the eighteenth and nineteenth centuries, the political situation of the Kirdi remained the same: marginal to the main political events, a slave reserve for the group in power.

At the start of the twentieth century the Fulani were defeated by the Germans and English. The Kirdi did not benefit from the defeat since the Europeans set up the Fulani Lamibé (chiefs) as local administrators. The colonizers had little choice in this. The Kirdi were so fragmented that direct rule was out of the question. This indirect rule greatly favored the Fulani. As administrators, they could utilize the military supremacy of the colonizers enabling them to subjugate Kirdi tribes which had previously eluded them. During World War I the Fulani were deprived of this external aid and the Kirdi attempted to take advantage. They stole cattle, killed Fulani and harrassed merchants. The Fulani retaliated with the modern weapons still at their disposal. An English colonial officer wrote shortly after the war about the western Higi territory:

> (these)... are (sic) the most lawless, ill-governed places I have seen in Nigeria since the early days of the Northern Nigeria Protectorate. Slave dealing and slave raiding are rampant.... Chiefs of minor importance were given rifles with which they were encouraged to attack the wretched pagans (who are) hiding like frightened monkeys on inaccessible hilltops.
> ... of course, everyone goes about fully armed: spears, shields, bows and arrows, clubs, etc., (Kirk-Greene 1958:84).

Only after the Second World War did the Europeans succeed in the pacification of the area. The Mandara mountains are quite isolated. Denham had discovered the mountains in 1823 and Barth had made note of them in 1852, but it took half a century before the first true exploration of the mountains was made. Captain Zimmerman made the first reconnaissance in 1905 (Dominik 1908:308) and he discovered the Kapsiki plateau. English exploration started in 1920. Pacification consisted mainly in ending the numerous wars between the villages. The last battles between villages (as described in the first chapter) took place well after World War II. In 1953 Mogodé and Sirakouti confronted each other for the last time on the battlefield.

It is hard to discern tribal units in the Mandara mountains before European contact. The first written information came from the Muslims, who found no reason to make a detailed study of their potential slaves. It is impossible to verify whether the Kirdi that fought against Bornu, Mandara and the Fulani were the direct ancestors of the Kapsiki and Higi who now live in these hills. It would be improbable, however, that the Kapsiki would have lived for centuries on the same spot. Oral history reveals a constant flux of population; village histories (tribal histories do not exist) are effectively histories of migration, tales about the places from which ancestors came. Most of the time, it was a small-scale migration. Villages were founded by few people coming from a place some kilometers away. The ancestral village often was situated within the Mandara region itself. The combination of continuous slave raids, intervillage warfare, and the scarcity of good cultivable plots probably gave rise to a constant flow of population within certain parameters. This internal migration prevented the formation of any intervillage political structure and enhanced the need for each individual to be self-reliant.

Even today any tribal unit is difficult to define. The language is almost as fragmented as the political situation and consists of a cluster of dialects with vague local village boundaries. At least eleven major dialect groups can be discerned within the Higi or Kapsiki language (Morhlang 1972). The cultural difference with the Margui (west), Sukur (north), Matakam (northeast) and Mofu (east) may be great enough to allow for demarcation; the Bana and Hina in the south are very much related culturally. In any case, the tribe as a whole has no great significance for the Kapsiki; a sense of ethnic unity is absent and ethnic loyalty unknown (van Beek 1986a).

Making a Living

The climate at this latitude of 11° north is dominated by the yearly rhythm of rainy and dry seasons. Rains may fall from June until September; the total precipitation seldom exceeds 900 mm. Heavy rainstorms normally mark the beginning of the cultivating season, although at the start of the wet season the rains occasionally may be so infrequent as to endanger the sprouting seed. Near the end of the cultivating season, the rains become more frequent and less violent. The dry season, from October through May starts hot, cools in December and January and grows very hot in April and May. In the valleys and on the Nigerian plain, the temperature can rise above 40° C. The mountain ridges and the plateau are cooler; shrub and low, thorny bushes form most of the vegetation. Throughout the savannah isolated accacias, cailcedrats, tamarinds, boababs and euphorbias add some variety to the otherwise monotonous shrub vegetation. Game is scarce due to high population density (40 to 70 per square kilometer) but some small antelopes, monkeys and foxes live in the more remote areas.

The Kapsiki cultivate their crops with great care and diligence in this mountain savannah environment. The hillsides have to be terraced with low stone walls to prevent water erosion. During the short rainy season people are extremely busy. Sorghum and corn are sown as soon as the first rains appear. The following month, in July, peanuts, tobacco, sweet potatoes, and sesame are sown or planted. The fields have to be weeded at regular intervals in the months of July and August. At the close of August rations grow short. Nights are cold and wet and much work remains to be done; it is a hard time for the people. September brings the first harvest: maize, followed by the fast growing varieties of sorghum. The remainder is harvested in October. After the harvest people stay busy building new huts, plaiting straw and threshing the sorghum. After December less water is available and most work has been done. In the following months, the main festivals and rituals are held.

Of all the crops sorghum is the most important by far. This staple crop is primarily consumed as *dafa*, mush, the main Kapsiki food. Another portion of the crop is used for beer, also an important item in the Kapsiki diet. The name Kapsiki or *kapsekE* means "to sprout." They let the sorghum grains sprout and make beer of the young tendrils, thus "Kapsiki," also means "Brewers." Other crops may be seen as complementary. Maize is the first harvested crop and so serves as food in the period of scarcity. Peanuts are important in sauces and dressings; in the field they serve as a rotation crop with sorghum and millet. On the few low-lying places where water is more abundant, cassave and yam are grown which serve as alternatives to sorghum mush. Sesame, beans, sorrel, couch, hibiscus and cucumbers are cultivated for use in the sauce. Tobacco is grown near the houses and used as snuff.

Most fields are situated on the mountain slopes; in former days this not only provided protection against surprise attacks but had an additional advantage. The mountainsides are easier to clear, as fewer weeds grow on them. The numerous stones must be cleared away and are arranged in little contour terraces. Once that has been done, the little patches of cultivable land can be used without too much trouble. Another advantage is water supply; rains and water supply are more dependable and stable in the mountains than in the lower-lying Nigerian plain. These advantages are crucial for a culture with a fully subsistent economy.

In recent times, after the pacification, the Kapsiki (or Higi as they are called in Nigeria) have progressed on the plains to the west. The produce of these fields fluctuates more than that of the mountain plots, but in favorable years they may yield three to five times as much. In cash crop production this advantage overrides those of the hill farms. Onions, potatoes, pepper and garlic have recently become important as cash crops in addition to peanut cultivation which had been the only source of cash income. The fast developing tourist trade had made the *rhwa* important. In

Kapsiki compounds on a terraced hillside.

little swamp areas near water holes, vegetables can be grown for the hotel in Rhoumsiki, producing a steady and considerable income for the cultivators of the plots. Cultivable land is not scarce due to several factors. The Kapsiki population, with a density of about 40/Km², is static; pressure on land is not increasing. Formerly, land was scarce. When only mountainsides could be cultivated because of slave raiding, good plots with adequate defense possibilities were in great demand. After the pacification the Kapsiki plateau and the Nigerian plains were opened up for cultivation and land has become a more plentiful resource.

Ownership of land was a simple matter of staking claim. Whoever claimed and used a new plot in the *gamba*, bush, for the first time, owned it. To claim a plot one had to sink rows of long stones to stake the field on one side; a riverbed usually formed the other boundary. At present, almost all cultivable land has been claimed: "there is no more real *gamba*" our informants emphasize. Today's farmers cultivate fields they have inherited or borrowed. Land is inherited patrilineally. After the death of the owner, it is divided between the brothers or sons of the owner. These same inheritance rules set certain limits to individual ownership. As a number of kinsmen have claims on fields, one should not sell one's fields. Many fields are loaned on a semi-permanent basis. Several people have inherited far more land than they can ever cultivate and about 50% of all Kapsiki cultivate on loaned fields. Close patrilineal kin can cultivate each other's fields without any compensation, but borrowers from other lineages or clans "pay" for the transaction with a jar of beer or with counterservice such as herding goats or cattle for the owner. This loan relationship implies no dependency or inequality and loans often occur between friends. Loans are inherited and may last for generations, resulting in great uncertainty as to actual ownership. Having cultivated the field for so many seasons the borrower many consider it to be his property, whereas the owner may not be too sure about his title. More often than not the boundaries have become unclear over time; a Kapsiki discloses the exact limits and boundaries of his fields only to a chosen few. Thus, at the beginning of the rainy season when cultivation is due to start, conflicts may rise over land titles. However, the number of conflicts over land is low since fields are not scarce. Other conflicts, like those arising over women and brideprices are far more numerous.

Ownership of land does not automatically imply ownership of the vegetation on it. Trees, a rare and valuable asset in this savannah country, are owned separately and individually, and are not included in loans of land. The owner usually comes down to cut the branches for his own use. Big trees are named after their owner. Newly planted trees, growing in the borrowed field are property of the borrower and remain his property after the field has been reclaimed. Two exceptions prove this rule: the *ndeweva* and the *sewe* (Zizifus Mauritania L. and Acacia albida Del.). According to

A field on the valley floor.

the Kapsiki they cannot be planted but grow at their own whim. The borrowers may cut their branches, but the trunk belongs to the owner of the field. If any paths cut across the fields, these are for general use and are not considered to be anyone's property. The same holds for water holes. Places with water are not owned but are common property. Access to them can not be barred. When a water hole dries up during the season of drought the new plot may be claimed. This gives rise to several conflicts, as some people may still consider it a well and thus, common property.

Livestock is also important in Kapsiki society and includes poultry, goats, sheep and cattle. The Kapsiki take pride in their own breed of short-horned, black-patched cattle, which contrast sharply with the long-horned, humpbacked stock of the Fulani. Cows are not milked by the Kapsiki, in fact, most owners do not even tend their own cattle. The Kapsiki entrust either a friend or someone among the nomadic Mbororo Fulani with the care of their beasts. In that case, the cows are milked and part of the milk is given to the owner. Goats and sheep are herded by small boys, often sons of the owners. The two main functions of husbandry are meat production and capital accumulation. At the weekly village markets at least one cow or ox is butchered. In the village of Mogodé this implies one ox a week for a village of about 2400 people. Other markets sell more meat but never abundantly. Any beast may be slaughtered for meat, but the occasion is usually a special one. Livestock is meant for brideprices, festivals, ceremonies and rituals. The only way for a man to stay married is to have a continual supply of beasts with which to purchase wives for himself or for his sons. Women also own cattle and use them to help their sons in getting wives or to help their husband with the brideprice of a new spouse.

In the traditional situation a brideprice is calculated and discussed in terms of goats with sheep being considered equal to goats. The value of a cow varies from ten to twenty-five goats. In recent years, money tends to replace livestock in brideprices and husbandry is slowly beginning to develop into market-oriented meat production. Currently only poultry is consistently raised for cash. Women raise chickens and sell the grown fowls at the market. In fact, poultry is far more important as a protein source in the daily diet than beef or goat meat. For the women, raising and selling chicken means a considerable source of cash income.

The differences in emotional value attached to livestock can be exemplified by the way of purchasing.

When someone buys a hen, payment simply ends the transaction. The purchase of a goat or sheep is a business-like transaction for the most part too, but not entirely so. Usually people sell these beasts to friends and relatives and keep themselves informed on the well-being of the animals sold. Selling cattle implies a more lasting relation. Cattle are sold to kin and friends in two possible ways, both involving a lasting relationship between the two parties. The first one needs a great deal of patience. One pays in advance for any calf to be born from a specific cow and then keeps hoping that a calf will be born. It may take years of waiting and both men remain in this relationship of dependency. Provisions are made for the untimely death of the cow or the birth of a bull-calf instead of the preferred cow-calf. The other way is to buy a living calf which is more expensive but entails less risk. When that cow has produced three or more cow-calves, it is returned to the original seller, "in order to return the luck." If the cow did not prove that productive, after butchering it, the horns and the sexual organs should be given to the original seller.

How important is this type of husbandry? For a horticultural society the Kapsiki own a considerable amount of livestock. About 1/3 of all adult men have one or more cows; a small minority owns more than five cows. An average Kapsiki household owns four goats and sheep; the distribution of this type of wealth is more even.

Compared to horticulture and husbandry, hunting and gathering account for only a tiny fraction of the diet. Women gather firewood in the bush, pick some leaves for the mush sauce or for salt (from the juniper tree), or dig some roots like that of Capsicum frutescens as shortening. Many other edible fruits and roots are known, but people use them only in times of crop failure and hunger. The indigenous medicinal system, however, is largely dependent on gathered specimens although usually not edible species. Hunting is of no great importance in the Kapsiki diet. Traditional oral history tells about elephants, leopards and buffaloes, but the present Kapsiki hunter encounters only small game like rabbits, guinea fowl, rats, mice and an occasional small antelope. In January and February of each year collective hunts are organized, but the yield is low. These hunting parties actually fulfill a ritual function rather than an economic one.

Co-wives threshing sorghum.

Organizing Work

Division of labor in Kapsiki society follows the traditional lines of sex and age, the first being the most important. Men and women have separate tasks in agriculture. Men clear the fields, arrange and repair stone terraces, grow maize, tobacco, garlic and onions while women tend such crops as peanuts, couch, red sorrel, beans and ground nuts. Sesame is a crop for young boys, associated with initiation. Sorghum and millet, the staple crops of the Kapsiki, are cultivated as a family enterprise by men and women; they are considered the husband's crops but his wives fully share the workload. Threshing is the woman's chore. The women beat the sorghum ears with large wooden flails and winnow in the steady January wind. The husbands transport the grains in big baskets to their granaries, singing songs of pride and happiness.

In other activities labor is also arranged according to sex.

Table 1: Division of Labor

	Men	**Women**
crops:	sorghum and millet maize tobacco sesame (young boys) sweet potatoes onions garlic	sorghum and millet (weeding, sowing and threshing) corn sesame sweet potatoes peanuts couch red sorrel beans ground nuts
other activities:	construction of huts cutting and plaiting of straw brewing red beer hunting herding cattle war	cooking woodcutting, cleaning fetching water brewing white beer

The great majority of tasks inside or outside agriculture are performed by the individual family or its individual members. A man grows some tobacco on his own, just as his wife has her plot of couch. Both join forces in sorghum cultivation which has absolute priority over any other crop. For a few agricultural tasks a bigger group is recruited. Cleaning the fields, terracing the hillsides and the difficult job of digging beds for sweet potatoes are performed by *meshike,* work parties. Whoever wants to have help with such a job picks a day, has his wife brew huge quantities of white beer, and recruits as many laborers as he can, calling in his neighbors, wardmembers, clansmen and friends. The total labor force he can command depends on several factors: his diligence in working for others, his stature as an important man in the ward and the village, his network of friends, the fame of his women as brewers, etc.

Starting very early at sunrise, the whole party lines up on one side of the field and works in a line towards the other end, with the true and steady workers marking the beat. At about ten o'clock women bring in jars of beer for a break. Usually the work is finished at about three in the afternoon, and all the workers assemble in the compound of the owner of the field, where the beer is hot and tasty. Using a strict drinking etiquette, everyone is filled to capacity and the following hours are filled with speeches by the village or ward chief, clan elders, and, later in the afternoon, by anyone who thinks he has something to say. This so-called *rhena za*, men's talk, may last till sunset.

Women have their own *meshike* for cleaning couch fields and for harvesting beans, couch and peanuts. They follow the same procedure, though the men take no part in it.

Work parties are also called for endeavors that affect the community. Although a house is built by the individual who is going to live in it, the porch of the house and the brewery have definite communal features and consequently are built by a working group. The same holds for building and repairing the ward smithy.

The Kapsiki food economy is largely self-sufficient with most of the produce being consumed by members of the production unit. Sorghum and millet, corn, groundnuts, couch and sorrel are stored in the granaries to be eaten at a later date. During the last decades the Kapsiki have been drawn into a larger market economy. About half of the sweet potatoes are sold and two-thirds of the onions, beans, and tobacco. Peanuts still represent the real cash crop; the cash income derived from peanuts amounts to about 60% of the total cash income of the compound. Self-sufficiency does not imply that every household grows all of its food. A considerable amount of produce is sold or bought at the market. Two aspects of the Kapsiki market may be discerned: the internal circulation of local produce and the import of externally produced goods with the concomitant export of cash crops. We shall call the first cycle the internal market and the second one the external market. The internal market distributes crops like sorghum, tobacco and sweet potatoes for the men, and sesame, hibiscus and couch for the women. Other items which change hands are wild honey (gathered by the women), meat, skins, straw-plaited granary covers, mats, ropes and sometimes wooden beds. All these are "male" products, sold and bought by males. All products of the smiths such as iron objects, bronze ornaments, pottery and medicine belong to this cycle too. In former times, when no regular markets were held, this whole cycle of distribution occurred between individuals meeting in each other's compounds; the blacksmiths' trade still follows this pattern. People who need particular objects simply look up the *rerhE* or make an appointment and have him make whatever it is they need. Payment may be in cash, sorghum, or iron bars.

With the advent of European colonization, weekly markets have been installed. They are aimed mainly at the external distribution cycle but

The "external" market in Mogodé.

stimulate the internal market as well. It has become far easier for a Mogodian needing tobacco to attend the Monday market than to seek out someone with enough surplus to sell. The market places are dominated by merchants from abroad selling clothing, shoes, dried fish, salt, soda, soap, kola nuts, pomade, blankets, matches, toilet water and perfumes. The last two items are bought by young boys eager to show off. All are externally produced and thus are expensive by Kapsiki standards. Blankets, kola nuts and perfumes are all items of conspicuous consumption. Other merchants, often representatives of large, government-controlled corporations, buy the Kapsiki cash crops at these markets. In the months of December and January crops of peanuts, onions and potatoes are sold at fixed prices. The government has set quotas for each trading house to buy for each cash crop. Later in the dry season, when the government quotas are filled, the same merchants buy these products for their own benefit, often at higher prices. Thus, most Kapsiki try to postpone selling as long as possible but are thwarted by the taxes which they must pay in December. In order to have the cash, many Kapsiki are forced to sell earlier at lower prices.

In the production of crops, the Kapsiki household operates as one unit only for a few vital tasks such as the cultivation of sorghum and millet. Generally a man and his wives conduct separate transactions and perform their economic endeavors quite independently. The master of the house supplies each of his wives with sorghum and/or millet for cooking and can expect some wives to hand him their peanut crop to sell (for his own benefit). As a rule a woman disposes of her produce herself. Whether she lets her husband sell her peanuts or not depends on her age and independence.

A young woman with some young children usually allows her husband to sell, in which case he will dispose of the money himself. When she grows older and more independent, without small children encroaching upon her mobility, a woman will probably handle her own trade. She may give cash loans to her husband (without expecting repayment), but she spends her income freely. These women sell pepper, sesame, couch, hibiscus and often peanuts. For their main source of income, beer and chicken, they are not in the least dependent on their husbands. In fact, the daily meals of a family may often depend on the wife's income from beer and chicken. Women deal on the external market more than men as they play a greater part in the cultivation of cash crops and tend to spend more of their monetary income on shoes, clothing for themselves and their children, matches, soap, salt and dried fish. Men tend to spend more on the internal cycle, selling goats and sheep, tobacco and carpentry and buying similar products. One remarkable fact in these transactions is the separation of the husband's activities from those of his wife. Both have separate budgets. Here are a few examples: a woman wanted a sleeping mat and bought it at the market. Her husband was selling exactly this type of mat at the market.

She would not expect the gift of a mat from him nor would she purchase one from him. The same is true for a man buying a chicken. He buys a chicken for dinner and presents it to his wife who has been selling chicken on the very same day. All purchases are made independently. Often both wife and husband buy identical items at the same place on the same day: whether it be soap, sugar, meat, hoes or hoe shafts. The man's budget is

Beer market.

about twice as large as his wife's, but her net gain may be on a par with his. Of his monetary income 50% is derived from selling crops and 37% from selling cattle. This money is spent on externally produced goods (30%), cattle (25%), carpentry and smiths products (18%). His wife spends her money differently—82% on the external market and 18% on plaited objects, carpentry, and smith's products; 71% of her income stems from selling beer and chicken, 29% from selling peanuts and other crops. A husband is fairly dependent on his wife for his wealth, either for production of the cereals on which the family subsists (the surplus of which he may sell) or for the production of cash crops which he may sell at her wish. A standard Kapsiki saying goes *male kawume rhungkE* or a woman marries (i.e. pays the brideprice for) herself. Moreover, loans are often given to a husband in order to woo and marry new wives. Old wives can be particularly instrumental in paying brideprice for new wives and the cycle repeats itself.

The Blacksmiths

Cultivation on the stony but terraced slopes is an arduous job in which the iron implement plays a vital part. Hoes, axes, sickles, adzes and knives are made in the village. The blacksmith, or *rerhE*, therefore plays a pivotal role. They are a small minority within Kapsiki society, comprising 5% of the total population. As an endogamous group, they form a close-knit subgroup with institutionalized relations of social inferiority with the main population. They are the specialists of the society. Blacksmiths forge iron, cast bronze, divine the future, heal the sick, assist in sacrifices, make music and bury the dead. They furnish the rest of the Kapsiki with tools essential for survival: agricultural implements, weapons, medicine and utensils.

Iron is wrought by only a few blacksmiths who specialize in that activity. The raw materials are available in the immediate vicinity: iron ore is found as magnitite in dry river beds. In the northern part of the Mandara hills an ample supply of iron ore has allowed for a primitive iron industry to develop. In the villages of Sukur and Mabass, just north of Kapsiki territory, a great number of people formerly engaged in melting iron and working it into iron bars. The blacksmiths from the southern villages forged those bars into the tools and utensils ordered by their clients. Today the melting of ore is rapidly disappearing, as iron from old cars and drums is readily available. Blacksmiths of various villages still forge tools and seem to compete with the externally produced tools imported by Hausa and Fulani merchants. The iron bars have lost their former function as limited purpose money, although they still serve as ceremonial gifts.

Iron melting is done in banco furnaces (see Lukas 1972) where air is preheated before being pumped into the fire. Preheating is accomplished by blowing the air through a vertical tunnel that descends straight into the fire itself. Pumping the air with the bellows is hard work, and people work in shifts at it, accompanied by blacksmiths on drums, guitars or little harps. The product, a crude mixture of reduced iron and charcoal, is reheated and forged many times to purify it before turning it into bars.

The village blacksmiths forge their products in low, roughly built huts, standing just outside their compounds. These smithies are built by the whole community since they are of communal interest. Inside them, a U-shaped oven of earth is fanned by a pair of goat skin bellows, blowing the air through a pottery tube. Stones serve as anvils and a hollow stone contains some muddy water for tempering. A special herb is added "to take away the wounds of the iron." A cone-shaped hammer, a poker and a pair of tongs are the only tools the smith uses. At the start of the rainy season, a man checks the condition of his implements. If they need repair or replacement, he goes to the smith's compound in the early morning carrying a basket of charcoal and several iron bars. He assists the smith at the bellows and his wives bring jars of beer throughout the day. He pays a few hundred CFA when the work is completed ($1.00).

To have special objects like medicine containers or iron sticks made, one has to arrange an appointment in advance. These objects require substantial time to make and the smith has to perform preparatory rituals. On his own initiative, the blacksmith may forge small articles like arrow points, spear

Smith Cewuve hammers the crude iron bar into a hoe, as the cultivation season nears.

heads, flint iron, tweezers and iron beads to sell at the market. Those blacksmiths who are prolific in iron forging earn a handsome living although these specialists still must cultivate their fields.

Not all *rerhE* products are of such practical use as the iron ones. Throughout the region of North Cameroon the "Kapsiki bronzes" as they are called, are well-known and sought after by tourists. This bronze is actually brass. In each Kapsiki village one or two blacksmiths specialize in brass casting. Using a "lost wax" ("cire perdu") method, they cast all types

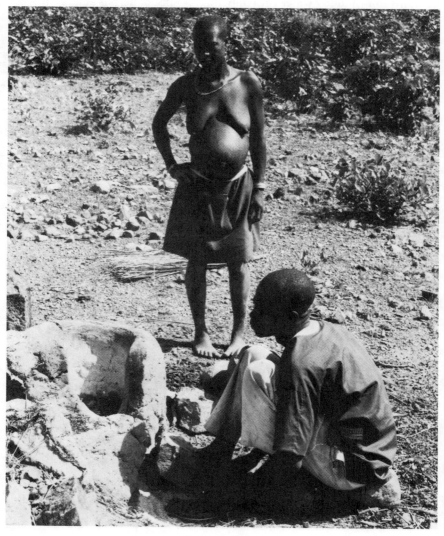

Brass casting.

of ornaments including bracelets, bells, beads, labrets, and rings. Other articles produced are: snuff containers, pouches, ceremonial sword sheaths and pipes. Ores are imported from afar, originating from South Nigeria. In fact, brass casting is a "southern art"; almost all smiths who specialize in it are immigrants from southern tribes. The casting itself is done in an open-air oven. The smith makes a wax model of the desired object and then covers the model with mud. He bakes the mud in a small fire, letting the hot wax drip out of an opening he has left. A pottery cup full of brass ore or brass waste is placed over the hole in the emptied mold; the cup and mold are heated in the oven, standing upright. As the brass melts, the smith turns the mold to let the brass run in. He then cools it in water, knocks off the mold and retouches the brass with a file. If he wants his product to have a reddish color, he may burn some straw in the oven while heating. The entire process is done by the smith himself. Clients do not help, although in some cases the smith's wives may assist. The smith supplies his own ore and charcoal. Brass objects are more expensive than iron products, and smiths who make them are generally well-off. Traditionally, bronze ornaments lasted a long time and demand was low, but recently tourism has created a huge demand for them, making brass casting a very profitable business for the few who practice it.

Pottery is made exclusively by the smith women in a great variety of shapes including bowls, jars and barrels. No wheel is used. The potter spirals a worm of clay into a circular shape, using a hollowed-out trunk as a mold. In some villages where a drier clay is found, bowls are formed by beating a lump of clay into the desired shape. The techniques are simple enough to enable all smith women to produce pottery. Most is made to order and the daily demand makes this specialty a small but steady source of income. Clay is plentiful in damp places near the villages.

Although the role of the blacksmiths in food production is crucial, many of their other activities contribute to the well-being of Kapsiki society. In general, they are the specialists of Kapsiki society. Any endeavor which requires a specialty is usually performed by a smith. Thus, the division of labor between the sexes and the ages is complemented by the division of labor between smiths and non-smiths or *melu*.

Smith	Non-smith *(melu)*
iron production	food cultivation
bronze (brass) casting	plaiting straw
pottery (women)	brewing beer (women and men)
burial	herding cattle
divination	hunting
music (drumming, fluting)	war
medicine	building
ritual assistance	performance of rituals

Of these tasks, ritually and socially the most important one is burial. Smiths are the "men of death"; this helps explain their inferior status in Kapsiki society. They are the undertakers—a job that is considered unclean, dirty. The caste-like character of their group probably stems from this association:

> When visiting a village on the border of the Kapsiki territory. We noticed all smiths had left that little hamlet. My friend's shocked reaction was typical: "What about the dead? Who buries your dead, or does nobody die around here?"

In burial the old smiths bear the brunt of the ritual work, while the younger ones supply the music and carry the body. The chief smith, the most important functionary of the group, oversees all proceedings of the burial ceremonies and performs the actual burial on the last day of the three-day festivities.

The smiths' work in burial is well-remunerated, either in food or in cash. A goat a day is standard for the old smiths, while the musicians receive considerable sums of money (1000 CFA per day, approximately $3.00). Keeping in mind the size of a Kapsiki village and the small proportion of blacksmiths (5%), both money and meat mean a substantial extra income for the smiths.

Music is closely associated with death, particularly drumming. All types of drums are played by the blacksmiths. Young smiths perform not only at burials but provide music at any function. Playing three-stringed guitars, banjos or stringed violins, the blacksmiths sing in the background of any large gathering of men. While other people drink and talk, the smith plays softly, singing praise to his host, to the chief or to anyone who presses coins on his forehead; he ridicules stingy chiefs and officials. A few musical instruments are used by non-smiths. Praise-singing, with its substantial revenues, however, is a smith prerogative.

Among some other groups in North Cameroon the troubadour role is even more striking. The singers there, called "griots" in French, constitute a separate caste. The most famous among them gain a large income from singing praise to functionaries, headmen and chiefs, as well as to descendants of former kings and emirs. The small bands of musicians and singers roam the countryside, residing at each and every chief's court. Marriages, independence festivals, circumcision, naming festivals and other festivities require griot songs. In the towns of North Cameroon they have become important in local and regional politics. Candidates for a certain post strive for massive griot support. Only if an adequate number of griots work and sing for them can they succeed in the regional political arenas. This, of course, is a modern development strictly tied to life in the cities. In the rural backwater of the Kapsiki village the praise-singing of the black-smiths is directed toward the village headman and the older and richer men

The troubadour blacksmith is rewarded for his entertainment.

(and sometimes toward the anthropologist who may or may not be old but is perceived as rich!).

Divination is the area in which the general intermediary role of the blacksmith is best illustrated. Any Kapsiki who needs to make an important decision or who is curious about what will happen in the near future consults one of the smiths who specialize in divination. Although there are several techniques which are considered valid among the Kapsiki, the most important one involves the crabfish.

Early in the morning the client arrives at the smith's house to "hear the crab." The blacksmith takes a pottery bowl filled with sand covered by a big potsherd, and fetches the pot in which he keeps his crabs. Some lukewarm water takes the chill out of the cold sand and creates a suitable environment for the animal. At the rim of the pot a series of grouped straws is put into the wet sand, representing the client and the social environment: kinsmen, wives, husband, the village, the burial place, etc. A dozen small pieces of calabash are put in the middle. Finally, the blacksmith puts the crab on top, after having told the beast why the client has come and what he wants to know. After covering everything with the lid, smith and client quietly chat away the quarter hour the crab needs to rearrange the pot, as an answer to the first question. After due time the smith opens the pot and examines the changes. He interprets the positions of the pieces of calabash, each having their own meaning. The answer suggests a new and more specific question; the whole procedure starts anew. The sequence of questions and answers frequently takes half a day. At the end of the session clients know why misfortune has fallen upon them, what further dangers the future holds, and what kind of sacrifices are needed to settle all wrongs and to avert all new dangers. The blacksmith is thanked with a shilling, the crab gets its grain of sorghum and the client goes home to perform the sacrifice.

In this whole procedure the smith is supposedly only a medium who simply interprets the signs given by the crabfish. In reality, a local smith knows the situation of his clients very well and reacts accordingly. In Chapter Four we shall see how this affects his relationship with his clients and how one of the main problems of Kapsiki society, the relationship between man and wife, is affected by the smiths' moderate control of supernatural information. This interpretative role gives the smith only limited power, since alternative diviners (including a few non-smiths) are always available.

Medicine and magic—two separate categories in western thought but not for the Kapsiki—form the most secret occupation. Blacksmiths are the main healers and magicians, a position which gives them status but which also segments them from the rest of society. Knowledge of *rhwE* is very secret and only transmitted between close kinsmen, from father to son, or mother's brother to sister's son. When ill, one seeks out one's habitual healer. In the middle of the night, the blacksmith in question gathers his herbs and roots and administers to his patient without anyone else being present. If the medication helps, the patient gives a handsome present, usually a goat or a sheep. If it does not help, the patient looks for another doctor using references from his close kinsmen and friends. Knowledge of medicine and magic (both are called *rhwE*) is very lucrative. A few smiths in the region have a huge reputation in magic.

Smith women have their own medicinal qualifications. They specialize in healing children—performing, for example, small operations on the anus. Some are renowned for their *kwante dewushi*, a technique to remove alien objects from the body:

> Kwarumba, a smith woman with a regional reputation in this technique has her patient kneel before her on hands and knees. Seated on a low stool, Kwarumba puts an old jar with muddy water between her feet. Having the boy kneel on hands and knees before her, she dips a few leaves in the muddy water and with strong, secure movements massages his belly. After a few minutes she suddenly straightens up and shows a

small frog, hidden in the green foliage in her hands. It bears the onoma-
topeic name of *kwankwErEkwE* and is considered dangerous. The
Kapsiki believe it enters the skin of people walking barefooted
through swampy areas. The only way to remove it is this particular
technique. In this session Kwarumba "removes" a dozen little frogs
from the child's belly. The treatment is repeated every morning, for a
fortnight.

This type of treatment — and its success — requires a comment. The idea
that illness results from the intrusion of alien objects in one's body is
one of the most common notions in tribal cultures, and can be found
world-wide. Stones, splinters, sharp bones, insects and even frogs are
thought to enter the body either by some kind of infection or by harmful
magic. A "magical" means of removal is called for. In no case does the
body show any signs whatsoever of either the intrusion of the object or
the operation. This trivial fact never detracts from the firm belief that
an actual object had entered and was removed.

The striking results of these "operations" are widely documented.
People do get better, because they believe in it, a psychosomatic reaction
well-known in western medicine. One might call this a placebo operation,
but with one proviso. All people concerned strictly believe in the procedure. The boy, his family and onlookers (this ritual has some show
elements) most assuredly believe in the diagnosis and treatment. The
specialist, in our case a smith woman, is more difficult to assess. Her act
depends on sleight-of-hand, a trick she has to have mastered and quite
consciously performs. There is no indication, however, that she
believes less than her clients. Anthropological literature corroborates
this: even in many instances where healers must use sleight-of-hand,
they still manage to believe not only in the efficacy of their treatment,
but also in its reality.

Not all *rhwE* can be classified as medicinal. All kinds of magic — a term
by which we indicate simple ritual directed toward a specific individual
purpose — are performed by the smiths. Examples range from gaining a
court case, to marrying a particular woman, to killing rivals, enemies or
kinsmen. When the latter occurs within the village, it is kept extremely
secret; someone using this kind of magic can be banned from the village.
Only the client will be removed. For a blacksmith, it is normal to know
about magic and to sell it.

Not all blacksmiths excel in every specialization, of course. Young smiths
might be musicians while the old ones lead the burial. Brasscasters or iron
workers might perform divination but probably would not engage in any
other activities, although they might play instruments not strictly associated
with death. Medicinal knowledge is not tied to any of these categories, but is
spread haphazardly over the smith population.

Beyond these specialist functions, the blacksmiths live as most Kapsiki do: cultivate their fields, marry women, beget children and try to be happy. Their social position in the village (their lower social status), however, does make a difference in everyday life. As much as their diaspora situation permits (they live dispersed throughout the village) they keep to themselves and try to keep the relation with the non-smith population as professional as possible.

The most telling difference in everyday life is the smith diet. No non-smith will ever drink or eat from the same vessel as a blacksmith, not wanting to pollute themselves. Blacksmiths do not share a great number of food taboos of the Kapsiki. The non-smith Kapsiki never eat horsemeat, donkey, tortoise, serpent, lizard and many other animals. All these are considered perfectly edible for the blacksmiths. Any Kapsiki caught eating a tortoise or serpent is severely chided by his fellow men: "Do you want to become a blacksmith, eating their food?" This notion is clearly expressed in numerous stories which relate that people turned into blacksmiths by eating the blacksmith food (van Beek 1982c).

The social inferiority of the blacksmith does not stop at the refusal of the other Kapsiki to eat with them. A smith is not considered fully adult. On public occasions, he has to sit in the background; his voice may only be heard in praise of the old men and chief of the village, either singing or clapping hands, softly shouting "Aya niveri" (well done, lion). His opinion is not heeded, nor is his experience called for. At a court trial a non-smith pleads for the smith, as he (or she) is the "child of the village," as a Kapsiki expression goes, never fully adult, never fully responsible.

The dependency of the smith on the rest of the population is highlighted by the fact that they have no kinship groups of their own. Each smith family is part of a non-smith kinship group. Of course, not being able to marry outside their caste, they can never truly be kin with non-smith, but they are adopted into the clan, a mechanism that we shall encounter in the marriage proceedings. Thus, every blacksmith has some kind of non-smith patron, someone who is responsible for the blacksmith, and to whom the smith bears allegiance. This patron is the one that speaks for the smith at public functions.

For some blacksmiths this overall social position too closely resembles slavery to be comfortable. A minority of the blacksmiths try to escape from their lower stratum — either by moving into the towns and adhering to Islam in the process or by becoming Christians in order to seek some upward mobility. Trades and crafts are open to them. The endogamy remains a hard and fast rule. The majority of the smiths, however, accept their position. In fact, they do gain some important advantages from being blacksmiths. In many ways the blacksmiths are better off than the rest of the population. They are better fed and command more cash than most Kapsiki. Blacksmiths' marriages are more stable than those of the non-smiths. Smith women do not shop around the marriage market as much as their non-smith sisters. On the whole, smith marriages last 50% longer than those of the non-smiths. Their infant mortality is about half of the general one, and the net replacement significantly higher:

Table 2: Demography of Smiths and Non-smiths

	smiths	*non-smiths*
gross reproduction rate	2.5	3.8
mortality before age 5	35%	67%
mortality before marriage	45%	72%
female sterility	17%	13%
net reproduction rate	1.05	0.95

Thus the smith population is slightly expanding, whereas the non-smith one is declining. Although the smith women give birth to less children (100 bear about 500 children, against 770 children for 100 non-smith women), relatively more smith children survive (van Beek 1986b).

Considering the individualistic attitude of the general Kapsiki culture and its tendency for equalization ("everybody is as good as anybody and quite a bit better") the two tendencies described above, — social deprivation versus economic and marital advantages — balance each other fairly well.

One important additional resource for any minority is cunning. Indeed, the cunning of the blacksmith is highly regarded by the other Kapsiki. Smiths are deemed to be the most clever people who easily fool the non-smith population. In traditional stories they are portrayed as the ones who see through any disguise and reveal the often unpleasant truth about their social superiors (see Chapter Six):

> This spectrum of smith/non-smith relations among the Kapsiki is in no way unique in Western or Central Africa. Throughout Africa smiths are considered to be very special persons who form either a lower or a higher stratum in society. Often they are just one of various artisan groups, sharing their pecularity with tanners, weavers, builders, praise-singers and so on. Even in that situation — which bears some resemblance to guild associations in the European Middle Ages — marriage within each group is strictly endogamic. The blacksmith's group is the most striking among the artisans. First of all, they are present in every society, even in the most remote villages since they are the ones who make agriculture possible. Secondly, they perform religious functions much more than the other artisans. Seldom are they religiously "neutral"; they are often associated with fertility and death, two notions that do not conflict in religion. The Kapsiki simply offer a very good example of this general smith situation; in their society the whole smith-complex with its endogamy, specific status, ideas of pollution, artisan specialties, intermediary function in ritual and magic, and association with both death and fertility can be seen very clearly.

3

Compounds, Clans and Clashes

As in any tribal society, Kapsiki life is structured primarily by the principles of territorial organization and kinship. People are grouped into a series of smaller and larger aggregates in order to regulate social and cultural life. Property and work, as well as ritual and marriage, are based upon those groups of kinsmen and neighbors. In Kapsiki society the largest relevant territorial unit is the village, consisting of a series of wards, which in turn consists of compounds. A village is based upon kinship; i.e., on a limited amount of patrilineal clans and lineages which cut across ward boundaries. The smallest elements of these are families and individuals. These divisions by no means co-exist harmoniously all the time. Conflicts do occur within the village. However, conflicts are regulated through descent and alliance rules. In our opening example, the infraction of one such rule called for war. The territorial and social structure with its concomitant conflicts forms the backbone of Kapsiki organization; it lies at the roots of the marriage system too. The monumental instability of Kapsiki marriage can be attributed to the hostility between villages, the divisions within the village, the rules of usufruct and inheritance through patrilineality and the bonds between co-resident males.

In our description of the social system we start with the smallest units, compound and family, and then proceed to the larger ones. While the information on kin groups is somewhat technical, it is highly important to understand the Kapsiki culture. Both clan membership and the claim to direct descent from the village founder are important for the rules of war and marriage.

A Kapsiki compound with huts and wall.

The Compound

The social unit "par excellence" in Kapsiki society is the compound. The Kapsiki term for it, *rhE* designates both the agglomerate of huts and the people living there; i.e., a family. In Chapter One the fortlike quality of the compounds was mentioned; indeed, an observer is struck at first sight by the fortified character. The main reason for this image is the *yindlu,* the man-high stone wall surrounding the huts and the highlight of Kapsiki architecture. The single opening in this wall leads into the house proper; it is marked by high stone pillars whose importance is manifest in ritual. Many chickens are sacrificed during construction and occupation in order to keep strangers and burglars from entering. Inside the wall, the entrance way leads through a two-door hut with a firepit which serves as a gathering place for the family in the wet season (see Figure 2). Beyond this entrance hut to the left, one encounters the man's hut surrounded by granaries. Behind these are the huts of his initiated sons. The brewery is built onto the wall at the rear of this male side of the house. If the man owns cattle, he may have some space on his side closed off as an open-air stable. Goats and sheep are kept in little low stables which form the base of the granaries.

Figure 2: A Kapsiki Compound in Some Detail

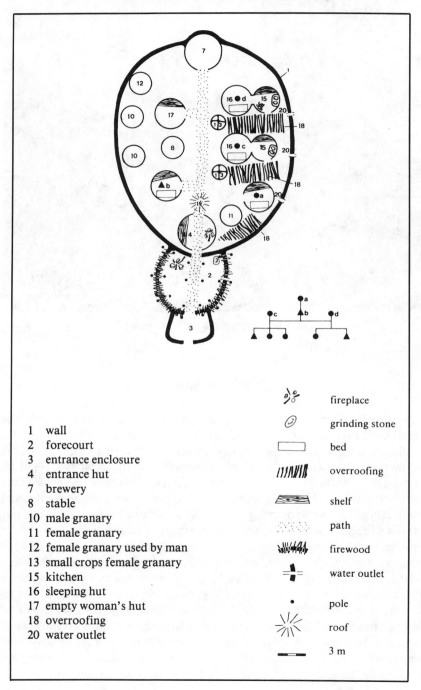

1 wall
2 forecourt
3 entrance enclosure
4 entrance hut
7 brewery
8 stable
10 male granary
11 female granary
12 female granary used by man
13 small crops female granary
15 kitchen
16 sleeping hut
17 empty woman's hut
18 overroofing
20 water outlet

fireplace
grinding stone
bed
overroofing
shelf
path
firewood
water outlet
pole
roof
3 m

View from the forecourt.

The female quarters, located on the right-hand side, are crammed with huts of the women, each having an adjoining kitchen and granary. In some cases a kitchen and a sleeping hut are built as one unit with a single entrance. The narrow spaces between the women's huts are covered with straw mats resting on wooden poles. Each woman has her own place to wash and perform her toilet, in the shade of these mats, with small waterholes leading through the wall. One or two huts are usually empty, as women come and go in a *rhE*.

Granaries, an important part of the compound in this agricultural society, are of several types. Men stow their supply of sorghum, millet and corn in cone-shaped structures made of mud or woven straw. There is an opening on top covered by a big straw cap. The granaries of women may resemble the male types or may be slimmer, in which case they are divided on the inside into small compartments. A woman's harvest consists of a number of different crops, including sesame, beans, sorrel and couch, each with a low total yield (van Beek 1986c).

One part of the house is situated on the outer side of the wall, the *derha*, or forecourt. This is the open-air gathering place of the compound in the dry season. A low stone wall (on which the firewood of the women is piled) surrounds it and a wooden structure covered with straw mats shields the resting family from the sun. This *derha* is the main setting for social functions as well as for family eating and resting. When neighbors or friends call, they are received in this room. Rarely do they visit other parts of the compound.

The orientation of the compound as a whole to the immediate environment depends on the position of the *derha*. The male side of the *derha*, on which the firepit is situated, should be the highest part; the side which is physically lower being reserved for the women. The division inside the wall follows the *derha*: the man's hut is built left from the entrance if the male *derha* side is on the left. The entrance of the *derha* should be lower than its exit leading into the compound. The symbolic value corresponds with the physical one: the highest place is the male side, the lowest is for the women, and the intermediate areas are for the young men and children (see Figure 3). The entrance of the *derha* should not be oriented east or west as the rays of the rising or setting sun should not enter it.

The term *rhE* stands for the inhabitants of the compound (the family) as much as for the house itself. Compound and people are one. Though some variation in household composition can complicate the picture, the model *rhE* consists of a man, his one or more wives and his children (offspring of either present wives or women who have left). Due to the great instability of

Figure 3: Plan of the Forecourt

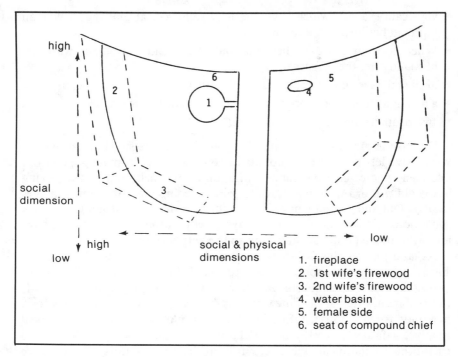

1. fireplace
2. 1st wife's firewood
3. 2nd wife's firewood
4. water basin
5. female side
6. seat of compound chief

Kapsiki marriages, many children are left behind to be reared by co-wives or kin:

> *Deli Kendeyi,* a man of about 42 years, has been married 3 times (below average for a man of his age). His first two wives have already left him. The first was with him for only one year when he was 23 and left him no children. He married the second one at the age of 30: she left 7 years later having born him two daughters and one son. His third wife, *Kwarumba Deli,* is still in his compound after a marriage of 8 years. She has given birth to three daughters and one son. Two daughters died in infancy. Thus in the compound of *Deli Kendeyi* lives a family with the following composition:

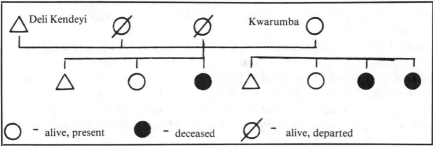

The most important residence rules are shown in this example:

- virilocality, a rule which is very strictly followed: at marriage a woman settles at her husband's compound.
- When a woman leaves her husband, her children remain with her husband after they are weaned.
- until marriage children stay with their father.
- a man may live in one compound with his old father or mother
- two brothers may live in the same *rhE*

Due to the mobility of women many adult men are single because their wives have left them. This amounts to 16% of the adult male population. Old men, who often are without a wife, may have their youngest son living in the old *rhE* or they might leave to join the compound of a son who lives nearby. Old and barren women return to their village of origin to live at a son's house. When an old couple stays together after all the children have left the house, a grandson may come to live with them.

As land for building is just as easy to obtain by loan as are fields in the bush, anyone can choose where to build his compound. The usual procedure for the establishment of a new *rhE* is quite simple: a newly married man, often at the time when his first child is to be born, looks for a new plot for his house. Often he chooses a plot near a close patrilineal relative, a father's brother or a FaFaBrSo. Brothers rarely build next to each other. Relationships between full brothers often are strained, as we shall see. Starting small, the compound will be enlarged in the coming years with huts for the new women he manages to marry, huts for his sons, stables for his goats, granaries and kitchens. The process is repeated when his sons marry. They may linger awhile in the compound but when they acquire more than one wife they usually leave to set up the *rhE* of their own, the older sons building at a greater distance from their father than the younger ones, while the youngest may stay with his father.

The establishment of a new *rhE* is accompanied by several rituals, most of them involving sacrifices of chicken. Representatives of both new and old wards participate in these rites. By drinking the ritual beer, they consecrate the building of the new compound. The construction of the entrance way with its high pillars and the completion of the forecourt are important events and are, therefore, ritualized. Each new completed granary is celebrated as well.

Daily life in the *rhE* depends heavily on the season. In the wet season the family functions as a working unit. In the early morning the wives soak some leftover mush in water for a quick breakfast. Before sunrise, man and children head for the fields, hoes in hand, small children on the backs of the older girls. The women go and fetch water, grind sorghum and cook new mush with a dressing of hibiscus, dried fish or chicken. When the cooking is

A storage hut is being built by a communal working party.

done they join the family. Everyone eats in the fields and continues to work until about three o'clock. Back home the family takes a rest, washes, drinks some beer and gathers around the fire to talk. The main meal of mush or porridge is served in the evening and all go to bed early. If she is very diligent or newly married, a woman might rise during the small hours of the night to grind the next morning's meal.

The dry season brings more variation in daily life. Men and women go about their separate business. The routine for the man is much less fixed. Shortly after the end of the rains he may be very busy building huts and cutting wood and straw for roofs. During the next months he may spend his whole day in his fields harvesting his sorghum or corn, or he might spend his day at the market selling his produce or his wives' peanuts. The wife's routine is less varied. She rises before sunrise to grind the day's meal, sweeps the floor of her hut and goes out to fetch water. Returning at sunrise she washes, heats some mush or cooks porridge, and eats with her children. If she is the only wife, her husband may eat with her too; if not, he is served separately. After the meal she goes out into the bush to cut firewood, usually together with some neighboring wives or friends. This is time-consuming as the women have to penetrate deep into the bush to find unclaimed trees; the whole party returns at noon. The family may eat some porridge at noon, but usually the Kapsiki eat only twice a day, at sunrise

Cooking sorghum mush.

and sunset. In the afternoon a woman may visit co-wives or friends, weave some fibers into a basket, or perhaps gather leaves for the evening meal. At sunset she fetches water for the second time and starts cooking. This meal is the main one and plenty of mush and sauce should be served. It is eaten around seven p.m. One or two hours later people retire to their beds and soon the whole village is sound asleep. When the moon is full, people may gather in the moonlight, talking and drinking, while the children dance in the eerie light, accompanied by the steady beat of the drums and the shrill sounds of various flutes.

Village and Ward

A distinct conglomerate of compounds is called a village or *meleme*. A village in the Mandara Kapsiki region is characterized by a well-defined territory, a proper name, a distinct political structure culminating in a village chief, a set of patriclans, and a specific tradition of origin. The traditional Kapsiki villages were situated on the mountain slopes for defensive purposes; for the majority of villages this is still the case. Since pacification, however, people have spread out over the plateau and the plains. In some villages, new wards have been created. Entirely new villages have been built as well. These new settlements often retain strong bonds with their ancestral habitat, but their composition may be quite heterogeneous. People from many different villages have gathered together to live in them. Despite this outward migration, the majority of villages are still arranged in the traditional way: a more or less dense settlement on an inaccessible hillside with surrounding fields and bush making up the village territory.

Villages vary in size from 1000 to 4000 habitants and each village is divided into a series of territorial subgroupings or wards, the number of wards depending on the size of the village. We shall describe one of the central villages, Mogodé, as a model.

Mogodé has 2400 inhabitants and is divided into 15 wards. One ward in the center of the village harbors all Islamized Kapsiki, drawn towards each other by the presence of the "chef de canton," a Muslim Kapsiki who is the representative of the local administration. The few Christians live together in a small ward near the mission station. The remaining 13 wards are traditional. The number of wards used to be much lower, but after pacification people went out onto the plateau and formed new wards. People from various clans and lineages (see below) live in each ward, although in some wards a concentration of one clan may be found due to the housing choices made by the clan members. Each ward has its chief, chosen by the village chief after lengthy deliberation with the old men of the ward; the appointment is authorized by the canton chief.

A man of any clan can become ward chief. Most *mblama*, as they are called, are recruited from among the young and ambitious. Someone who likes to become *mblama* gives frequent beer parties and woos the village headman with gifts. The old men do not relish the work of the ward chief: collecting taxes and party subscriptions, distributing identity cards or rounding up the inhabitants of a ward to work on the roads. Some aspects of the title compensate for the duties. A *mblama* is always the honored guest at a beer party, and he has a say in the immigration of a newcomer to the ward. In rituals he may fulfill an important role. People expect him to be diligent, generous and open-handed. He should guarantee the old men immunity from taxes, pay the party membership for a few poor people and give beer parties frequently. As the Kapsiki dislike any interference in their private affairs, whether from government or private citizens, the work of the *mblama* is often very difficult. Work on the roads, voting for a new constitution or attendance at a national festivity create no problems if the

A gathering place in a ward.

traditional concluding festival—a beer party—is held. Paying for official documents and taxes is a wholly different matter. Worse still are the reforms the government may want to impose. The governments of both Nigeria and Cameroon forbid fighting, prohibit the use of magic in the courts, and try to regulate marriage instability. They have also banned *caca,* a game of chance. The implementation of these measures can cause a ward chief to run into problems, as the following example shows:

> After a ritual beer party the men of one ward were gathered in a compound. The ward chief, *Kweji Hake,* was accused of allowing people to play *caca* after the weekly market. He did not deny this accusation, but defended himself in the following way: "People who look for trouble are not those who play *caca.* The onlookers come to drink beer and make trouble. Those at the game do not fight. I have nothing to say. Do you see any gray hairs on my chin? (i.e., I am young, many of you are much older, so how can I prohibit someone in the ward). As for me, I am tired of this headmanship. I have gained nothing from it. Beforehand, I cultivated a lot, enough to pay for the initiation of my brother and for my sister's marriage. Now that I am *mblama* I have no harvest. I am starving. Everyday you see me walk with a calabash to buy millet. I am given the party cards to distribute, and I distribute them correctly. Yet people say: 'He has not given to his father; he has not given to his father-in-law.' I know I did the right thing. People say: 'He pays no taxes; his father pays no taxes' and yet I see all my money disappear in taxes for other men. I have lost 500 CFA with those membership cards and I have had it. I am quitting. When people whispered that I was corrupting our children by allowing *caca,* that really hurt me. It was the last straw. If they want to play *caca* in front of my house, I'll give them a mat to sit on. They say I corrupt the village, but I see that those players do not steal and I will not forbid them to play. I have had enough."

The village chief or *maze meleme* is by far the most important functionary in the village. In fact he acts as the representative of the whole village with either government officials or the supernatural world. His main traditional task is a religious one, *kahi meleme* as it is called in Kapsiki, "to heal the village." *Maze* should run the village in such a way that no supernatural sanctions befall his people. The blacksmith diviners are consulted at frequent intervals, and are asked about imminent dangers and possible catastrophes. The chief then sacrifices according to the instructions to ward off "evil things." When public rituals are to be performed, he walks through the village in the falling dusk warning everybody of the "hot day" that lies ahead and exhorts his people to follow the customs, to "let the hoe lie at their side" (no one should work on fields while important rituals are held). He plays a vital function in many important rituals; in fact, in all rituals aimed at the general well-being of the whole village, *maze meleme* is one of the central officials, the obvious mediator between the village and the gods.

His political tasks, also called *kahi meleme*, rely for their effectiveness upon the authority the chief has as a religious mediator. In other words, the chief has no access to political sanctions to arrange matters in his village. He is respected, not obeyed. When he coordinates the administrative tasks of the *mblama* he encounters the very same problems, but as *maze* he is a little better equipped to cope with them. As a mediator he should be a true example for all villagers, a paragon of Kapsiki virtues. Not only does he remind his people constantly to heed the rules and conform to the central values of Kapsiki life, "work hard, do not quarrel and do not interfere with others," but he should exemplify these virtues even when the odds are turned against him. The chief of Mogodé once described the chiefly attitude as follows:

> If you are chief, you are so because the people love you, and they do so because you are soft and smooth, just like cotton. People do not say, "I will give him such and so because he is hard and troublesome." On the contrary, people give because one is friendly and generous....
>
> As a chief you are like a rubbish heap, who receives with equanimity what is thrown upon it, without offense or retort. If one puts faeces on the heap, does it spit back? No, it cannot even say that it is insulted. A chief just laughs when he is pushed to and fro and goes home without ire.

This peaceful reaction runs counter to Kapsiki attitudes. They normally react fiercely to perceived wrongs, but a chief cannot afford to let his personal character intrude. As a functionary and mediator he is a non-person, whose social role dominates his everyday behavior. Thus he follows rules of social behavior very strictly. He also has to conduct himself according to a set of specific rules applying only to him. He may not stay in another village after sunset and should remain inside the village territory as much as possible. He should not walk through the village by himself but should always be accompanied by his assistant (see below) or other notables. When death strikes his immediate family he may not wail too loudly nor shed visible tears. If his wife happens to run away he cannot seek her in her new village (as the husband did in our opening case), but sends her son or a friend in his place.

The village people should behave respectfully towards the chief, seeking him in his compound with small gifts or applauding his talks in the *rhena za*. The blacksmith have a special bond with *maze*; their headman is consulted frequently by *maze*, and the musicians among the blacksmiths hold occasional serenades to laud him. Despite this etiquette, it can be quite difficult to distinguish a village chief in daily life and labor. He cultivates his own fields, builds his own huts and exerts himself to marry and then to keep his wives because they wander freely just like anyone else's wives.

In order to become village chief a man must be of correct descent and have been chosen by the old men of the village. Among the various patrilineal clans in the village, one clan holds the key to the chieftainship, one of the clans that claims direct descent from the original founder of the village. This *maze* clan (literally chief clan) furnishes all candidates for the position, often amounting to two or three possible options. From among these clansmen the old men of the village choose one who is considered best suited to the rigors of the headmanship. He should have the proper attitude toward public welfare, so the old men pick someone who cares more about the village than about his personal well-being, who has a keen eye for injustice and a tongue able to offer advice. When the choice is made, an elaborate installation ritual follows, in which representatives of the various clans of the village participate. This ritual is significantly similar to a burial rite. The chief-to-be has to lose his own personality *(mehele)* in order to represent the village as a whole and to mediate with the supernatural world or, in a Kapsiki saying, "The man must die to live as a chief."

After his installation, the new chief chooses a friend as his assistant *(tlewefe)*, someone who will always be at his side on official occasions helping with administrative tasks, a partner to drink with at beer parties and festivals. Both choices have to be authorized by the local governmental representatives, such as the "chef de canton" in Cameroon and the district chief of Chubunawa district in Nigeria.

Patrilineal Groups

All people living in a Kapsiki village are part of one of a set of patrilineal clans which belong only to that village. The Kapsiki term for a clan *kayita* (literally people of one father), can be applied to a patrilineal group of any size. The sons of one father, the descendants of a patrilineal ascendant four generations removed, or all those claiming patrilineal descent from the mythical ancestor whose supernatural exploits gave birth to the village, can all be called *kayita*. Clans bear names, of their founders mostly, and so do the lineages into which the clans are divided. The majority of clans are divided into three lineages. Inside a lineage common descent can be traced exactly and rules of exogamy are followed strictly. Distant kinsmen cannot be traced precisely within whole clans as the genealogy has gaps in the upper region. Clan members from different lineages may marry but this is not a preferred union.

Segmentation of lineages occurs at several levels. Two levels—lineage and clan—bear names, but these two do not exhaust the possibilities of division. A minor lineage, which is important in social life, consists of all patrilineal descendants of FaFaFaFa, and is often named after this ancestor: "the sons of so and so."

Teri Kuve helps to divide the goats slaughtered for the occasion; a gathering of his lineage at a twin festival.

On the village level, all clans are grouped into two phratries, loose clusters of clans bound together by an idea of common origin. They are unnamed and, of course, not exogamous. For this twofold division the apposition "aristocratic" versus "commoner" has been coined (Smith 1969:36) but the relationship of these phratries is not hierarchical enough to warrant that distinction. The representatives of the so-called aristocratic clans do have a special function in the installation ritual of a new chief and in the yearly initiation ritual of boys. The spears of these boys are placed in a somewhat higher place, but that is about all. Phratries function mainly in internal war. Most violent conflicts within the village occur between these two groups (See Figure 4). We shall simply refer to them as the first and second phratrie. For Mogodé this division of phratries, clans and lineages works out in the following manner:

Figure 4: Clan and Lineage Organization

Phratry 1		Phratry 2	
clan	lineage	clan	lineage
maze	maze		makwiyE
	hweteve	makwiyE	kumbi
			sunukuvekwanyE
	majiwedawa		makwamte
ngacE	jirivi		gwenji
	shilEa		mava
	rhwaba		
makwajE	pakelE	zeremba	
	jEwu		

These clans and lineages form the backbone of village social organization. In fact the central myth of Mogodé which "charters" the origin and foundation of the village explicitly states the causes for phratry and clan organization as well. As is the case in nearly all Mandara mountain tribes, these myths center around migration histories which are voiced in kinship idiom. A village is founded by the first immigrant with his family; his sons constitute the clan ancestors; their heroic deeds, quests, strifes and struggles make up the core of village oral tradition. These myths concentrate on the village as a social unit. Although we shall discuss some myths bearing on relationships between villages later, the village history remains the focal point of interest. For Mogodé this is as follows:

> The first Kapsiki came from Goudour. After settling in Mogodé, they became numerous. An enemy grew afraid of their numbers and tried a trick. He told them: "If you see a red light coming from the *Nzambe* mountain (east), go and hide yourself in that cave." When on the following day they did see a red fire on *Nzambe* (the rising sun), they all flocked into the narrow cavern. The enemy, who knew the caves well, put a heap of straw in front of the entrance, set fire to the pile and blew the smoke into the cavern. All inside succumbed to the smoke except a certain *Ngwedu* and his sister who, by tying leather bags around their necks, saved themselves from suffocation. After two days the two of them left the cave and looked out over the desolate plateau dotted with volcanic outcroppings. They were searching for a living human being, but there was not a single soul in sight. They climbed an outcrop-ping, thereafter called *Rhungwedu* (the head of *Ngwedu*), cutting thorny bushes on their way up. From the summit they saw fire in Gouria (a neighboring village). After some discussion with his sister, *Ngwedu* went down to get some fire which the people in Gouria gave him on one condition. This was that the head of every cow *Ngwedu* would slaughter in the future and the head of every goat that he or his children would kill would be presented to the people of Gouria, who had made it possible for them to survive. *Ngwedu* accepted the fire on these conditions and went back to his sister. They lived together and their first son was *Teri Dingu,* who in turn begat *Hwempetla* (the main mythical culture hero of Mogodé). *Hwempetla* fathered six children. His first wife gave birth to three boys, *Maze, NgacE* and *MakwajE* and his second wife brought forth *MakwiyE, Makwamte* and *Zeremba.*

The Kapsiki are not overly interested in the mythical charter of their clans. Their main focus in mythology is the person of *Hwempetla*, mentioned above, whose exploits are narrated with gusto and in great detail. The origin of the village (which precedes him) and the division into clans and lineages coming after his great and mighty quests get less attention.

Lineage fission is an ongoing process. The factor determining fission is the size of a clan or lineage. The average number of adult men in the first three clans in Mogodé is 67, with 26 in the respective lineages. When a clan harbors about 55 adult males, fission is due. One example in Mogodé is the *makwamte* clan numbering 60 *rhE* heads. This clan is still undivided but hovers on the brink of fission. *Makwamte* members tend to use additional specifications to indicate clan members: "My brother Teri, one of the sons of Kwevi Kweda," which means belonging to the future Kwevi Kweda lineage. Our informants explicitly state that "the clan is too big." One additional factor in fission and naming of lineages is the presence of dominant ancestors after which the lineages may be named.

The smallest patrilineal group, the sublineage, in daily life is the most important. This group, comprising all patrilineal descendants of a male ancestor three or four generations removed, is an informal but effective corporate unit. As close agnates its members frequently interact, often living near each other. This group is consulted for all important decisions, such as the preparation of a marriage or the sale of property, and in all social events these agnates are among the first to be invited. Their most important task is to control and exploit their member's property. Though rights for usufruct of fields in principle reside in individuals, the members of this sublineage are each other's potential heirs. Thus, sale of any property that could be inherited, such as cattle, medicine, textiles, weapons and — in recent times — land is of interest to all of them. Whenever an important transaction in cows or land is about to be contracted, the older men of the sublineage may feel sufficiently motivated to overcome the usual Kapsiki restraint to tangle with someone else's business, in order to keep their eventual property intact.

Although the importance of patrilineal groups in Kapsiki society is curtailed by the high value put on individual autonomy and self-sufficiency (in Chapter Six we shall dwell more extensively on this topic), the patrilineal system forms the backbone of social structure within the village. Without *kayita* one has no "brothers" and without brothers life is lonely and insecure. Clan membership, to start with the largest *kayita*, is a label. People are referred to as members of such and such a clan, and then define their own identity in terms of clan affiliation. One classifies one's co-villagers by means of the largest relevant social group, and in many cases this is the clan. All clan members may be referred to as *wuzeyitiyeda* (son of my father). Thus the main function of the clan system is to organize the amorphous mass of village people into a set of distinct, recognizable and identifiable groups of convenient size and fixed composition. People determine their social niche in this way.

Clan stereotypes help reduce the complex reality to a more simply perceived social environment. Clans often bear the image of their name. Thus the *makwamte* (literally brothers in the bush) are considered to be the real hunters and prolific warriors and are people of the great outdoors. The *ngacE* (literally build a house) are said to be the master craftsmen in building huts and granaries. Within the clan the lineages are viewed stereotypically too: the *majirivi* would be the fierce people, warlike and quarrelsome, whereas softer and more peaceful people should be looked for among the *majiwedawa*. All this, however, remains just a stereotype and has little foundation in reality. The Kapsiki clans do not form a system of specialists nor do they present an incipient division of labor, as has been suggested in some publications (e.g. Hurault 1958). All Kapsiki build their own houses

Sacrificial jars of a lineage.

and in any clan good hunters, good building craftsmen are found just as well as bad ones. The one and only social group of specialists is the *rerhE* group, the blacksmiths.

Social identity, ceremonial positions and stereotypical characteristics are tied to lineage membership. The *shilEa* lineage, for example, of the *ngacE* clan furnishes the main officiator in the village *(mnzefE)* and the functionary who enthrones the chief is from this lineage. In a few instances the lineage may function as an economic unit, mainly when one member runs into huge debts. The price for a killing is one instance of this, but unpaid brideprices can become lineage business too. However, sub-lineage and compound are far more important economically. The primary function of clans and lineages is to give their people an uncontested place in society. This clearly shows during those times in which people act as members of a group, for example in ritual and war. Here we shall briefly consider the function of clans in ritual and later dwell more extensively on war.

Clans are represented as a whole in rituals by a true descendant of the clan founder, chosen, with the consent of the village chief, by the old men of the village and clan. This representative is just that, a representative. He has no official function in the clan and bears no authority over it. He may be replaced at the clan members' wish. He and the representatives of the other *ndegwevi* (non-immigrant) clans assist the village chief (who represents the *maze)* and the chief blacksmith in performing sacrifices twice a year for the well-being of the whole village. Representatives may serve in the installation ritual of a new village chief. Some division of labor is to be found in these ritual functions: the representative of the *ngacE* clan leads in the village sacrifice and in war-rituals and bears a special title. In fact, this sacrifice is the re-enactment of a sacrifice in the ancestral compound, and the representatives stand for the sons of the ancestors of the various clans or lineages.

At the start of the rainy season, a ritual hunt aiming at rain is led by *maze peli,* master of the hunt, a representative of the *makwajE*. The *nderigi,* (master of the bow), leads in some war rituals. He is a *gwenji* man. Among these ritual tasks that of *maze meleme*, village chief, is, as we have seen, the most important by far. He acts as representative of the entire village as well as of his *maze* clan. Lineages are represented in ritual in a similar way:

> The lineage sacrifice of the SunukuvekwanyE may serve as an example of this representation of the *kayita* by its members. As an immigrant lineage, its own rituals are performed apart from the main village sacrifice. These take place under an overhanging hillside, with the sacrificial jar, a few calabashes, some sticks and some soda hidden from curious views. Sacrifices are performed in January and June, following the genealogical order of the clan (see genealogy below). *Menu* brews the ritual beer, while *Ntake, Kweji, Derha* and *Kwada KwanyE* provide the sorghum flour and officiate in the sacrifice. The same lineage is responsible for another sacrifice on a different hilltop in which *Deli 'Yima* slaughters a red cock. The genealogy shows why: the first sacrifice reunites the descendants of *Sunu Kuve KwanyE,* the "children" of *Kweji Kuve KwanyE* being cared for in the second ritual.

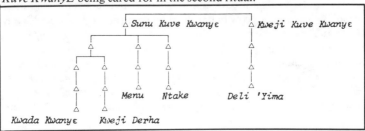

In some rituals the clans are not merely represented by one person, but
actually do unite and act as one group. At the concluding dance of the great
annual feast (see Chapter Four), all men of one clan dance as a group,
showing off their newlywed wives, while the clans are grouped according to
the phratries. At another occasion, the funeral dance, hoes, calabashes,
quivers and iron skirts symbolize the relationship of a dancer with the group
of the deceased; in initiation ritual all boys of one phratry put their spears
on the same spot, well-separated from the other half.

Most lineages and clans, as we have seen, claim descent from the culture
hero *Hwempetla*. Often this is a pious fiction as actually a minority of the
people of Mogodé can claim genealogical descent from their village
founder. There are two reasons why people may not be able to claim
autochthonous descent. In the course of history people have immigrated
from other villages in two fashions. First, whole clans and lineages have
joined the descendants of *Hwempetla* at *Rhungwedu*, finding their way into
the fabric of Kapsiki social life. Most immigrant clans and lineages
wandered in the direction of Mogodé in the early days of the village. The
second path is individual immigration. First an example of the collective
kind. The ancestor of the *gwenji* clan, according to oral tradition, came in
the days of *Hwempetla*.

The battle against Gouria stands out among the many exploits of
Hwempetla. He is soon fed up with the dependency on Gouria and breaks
the rule of returning heads of slaughtered cattle. War results, a war in which
Hwempetla and his brothers exhibit some marvelous shooting, but to no
avail. Although all their arrows find their target, no Gourians die. At the
crucial moment *Gwenji*, a stranger, appears on the scene with a huge
buffalo horn full of poison. He is welcomed as a savior, poisoned thorns are
scattered throughout the battle field, and as the Gourians try to pursue the
fleeing Mogodians, they tread on them and die from the poison. From that
time, *Gwenji*, called *Gwenki rhwE* (poison) by most, is established in the
village of Mogodé, and so are his descendants.

Immigrant groups may serve as lineages in existing clans too. In Mogodé
such is the case for the *SunukuvekwanyE* and the *Kumbi* lineages. In both
cases myths charter the special relation between that lineage and its host
clan. The *Kumbi* myth is a typical example:

> *Kumbi*, ancestor of the lineage, lived in a village in Nigeria where all his
> wives brought forth still-born children, so he made plans for migration.
> His loins girded with a cow halter, he showed up at the *Hwempetla* com-
> pound in *Rhungwedu* and coughed to call attention. *NgacE*, one of the
> *Hwempetla* children was sent out to see who was there, but being a lazy
> boy he just said that nobody was in sight. The second child, *Maze* (ances-
> tor of the *Maze* clan) was no better and then came *MakwiyE*. He
> received *Kumbi* cordially, inquired as to his circumstances and after
> hearing his plight, invited him into the house and gave him food and

shelter. After a few days *Kumbi* went back to Nigeria to fetch his belong-
ings and returned with an enormous herd of cattle, sheep and goats.
Then the other children were anxious to receive the guest, but the whole
wealth was to be *MakwiyE's*. A fight followed between the ancestor of
the first and the second phratrie, but *Kumbi* intervened on behalf of
MakwiyE and was definitively accepted as his "son."

This same example shows the procedure followed by individual
newcomers, the second type of immigrant. Notwithstanding the insistence
on autochthony and the permanent image of the fortified Kapsiki
homesteads, migration occurs frequently. Most emigration is small scale,
from village to adjoining village. Whoever wants to move contacts a friend
in the new village and makes his home at his friends *rhE*. His host then
furnishes him with a plot to build his compound, with fields to cultivate and
in all other respects acts as his social father. The newcomer is automatically
adopted into his host's clan, as his son, making for such a smooth transition
that after a few generations his descendants may not be aware of immigrant
status any longer, although they technically remain immigrants.

Both types of immigrants are called *kanza* "they who stay," and their
status is somewhat lower than the *kagwevi*, who can trace descent from the
village founders. The latter drink the ritual beer first, lead the dance in the
annual rites and may officiate in village sacrifices or provide the sacrificial
food. No immigrant *maze* should become village chief, and at burials of
kagwevi a small additional ritual is performed. The difference mainly shows
in ritual matters. In most daily activities the immigrant status makes no
difference at all and *kanza* operate as full-fledged village members.
Nevertheless, people are sensitive to this distinction. Enquiry into *kanza*
status is not welcome. If immigration occurred many generations ago,
people prefer to have others believe they are *kagwevi*. When our
investigation showed that only one-third (145 from 440 adult males) could
claim *kagwevi* status, people were shocked: that many *kanza*!

What are the social consequences of this immigration for the fabric of
social groups within the village?

The second phratry on closer inspection harbors far more immigrants
than the first one (177 versus 118 immigrant adult males), due not to
individual newcomers but to the immigrant clans. What happened in the
course of history and what are the charter myths trying to tell us? Without
immigrant clans, the numerical balance between the two village halves
would be disturbed. With the immigrant clans the balance is far more even.
The point is that both village halves often fought each other, in fact they
constituted each other's favorite enemy. In these internal village conflicts,
as we shall see, the fact of fighting itself is more important than its cause, so
a balance of power was necessary. The myth thus tells us that the reason
why the newcomers joined the ranks of the second phratry was to keep up
its fighting strength. Though this message is well-hidden in the Mogodé

myth, in other villages people have performed similar acts quite explicitly:

> In the village of Rhoumsou, north of Mogodé, oral tradition has it that
> one whole clan had been shifted to the other phratry in order to have the
> balance restored. The chief clan became too numerous and the old men
> of the village decided to change the loyalties of a small clan toward the
> "enemy."

War

In our opening case we saw two villages fighting each other. This kind of
war was quite important but by no means constituted all Kapsiki armed
conflicts. Within the villages clan fought against clan, phratry against
phratry and ward against ward. A word of caution before delving into these
conflicts. Warring between villages and fighting within villages has
diminished since the pacification of the Kapsiki area, which began about
twelve years after World War I and was completed only well after World
War II. The battle between Mogodé and Sirakouti, as described in Chapter
One, took place in 1953 according to oral information and was the last full-
scale war of both Mogodé and Sirakouti. Other villages report about the
same pattern. Thus, all accounts of fighting stem from oral tradition and we
have observed no war going on. However, although fighting may have
diminished, it has not completely ceased. During our field stay people from
Kortchi, a village in the bush on the eastern fringe of the Kapsiki territory
where life has changed even less than in a central place like Mogodé,
launched a massive attack on Vindé Gawar, a neighboring village of mixed
tribal composition (Kapsiki, Mofou and Fulani). With a party of some
twenty men they ambushed a group from Gawar going into the fields, killed
one man and abducted a woman. "Like the old days" my informants
gloated. They were delighted with the news, revelling in the fighting itself,
while at the same time believing that the inhabitants of Kortchi were
"dangerous savages."

Although the days of fighting are over, fighting ability and fierceness are
still important values in Kapsiki society. A real *za* (man) should be aggressive
and self-assertive and should resort to arms if needed. Acts of bravery draw
general admiration, and tales about former heroic exploits and dangerous
deeds never cease to fascinate old and young alike. Often during a beer
party or a men's talk (*rhena za)* someone recounts the wars of the past.
Using the vast ideophonic resources of the Kapsiki language and a
stupendous array of gestures, the narrator transforms the story into a
lively show: arrows whistle through the air causing shouts of pain and
whoops of triumph while all listeners (and spectators!) are bent double with
laughter hearing how a village member whined after an arrow found its way
into him (especially if that village member is still living and present). On

these occasions a quirk of Kapsiki humor shows: they cannot see other people suffer without a hearty laugh! More important for us in this respect are the social consequences of endemic warfare; in fact the organization of the clans and phratries within the village and the system of secondary marriages are only to be understood within the framework of intravillage conflicts and intervillage hostility. In other words, war has until recently functioned as a major structuring principle of Kapsiki social and matrimonial organization. On the other hand war has been largely the result of these same social and matrimonial systems, thus forming one interrelated system at the core of Kapsiki culture.

The Kapsiki have a gradually escalating system of violence in which the use of weaponry correlates with the social distance of the parties. In case of close kinship between the opponents a few non-lethal weapons are used, but in the absence of kinship bonds protagonists have any weapons at their disposal. Though one may postulate several intermediate categories in warring (Otterbein 1968:201), for our analysis three levels will suffice:

Table 3: Armed Conflicts

native term for type of conflict	opponents stem from:	weaponry used:			mediation through:
		wood	iron	poison	
1. *mpa cE*	same lineage or clan	x			clan members
2. *mpa derha*	same village — different clans, wards or lineages, or related villages	x	x		village chief *mnzefE*
3. *mpa te mpa* or *rhwebe*	different and non-related villages	x	x	x	daughter's son

The first type of conflict, between members of one *kayita*, remains a private affair. When two kinsmen disagree fiercely and try to force their arguments by pounding on each other's heads with a wooden club, the older members of their *kayita* are very quick to separate them. Even if they belong to different lineages, the idea of corporate unity is sufficiently strong to prevent the lineages from rallying behind the combatants and engaging in a corporate fight against the other lineage. No iron weapons may be used in such a duel and our informants quite emphatically stated that no one would dream of violating that rule. Wooden clubs are the appropriate instruments. If one should wish the death of a clan brother, other means offer themselves for that end, such as sorcery. As we shall see, clan brothers and full brothers may in reality often be at odds, but these conflicts should never come into the open.

The next type is clearly differentiated from the former by its native name. *Mpa cE,* the conflict within one clan, means literally "fight in the hut," whereas the translation of *mpa derha* is "fight in the forecourt." In the latter cases, individuals commence the hostilities and the groups to which both men belong rally behind their champions and fight each other as a group. So all men of one ward, clan or phratry fight the men of another ward, clan or phratry. In such a fight iron weapons are allowed but no poison may be used; i.e., no bow and arrows. Knives, swords, spears and *ngalEwa* (slashing knives, sometimes dubbed "throwing" knives) may freely be used.

Such a fight starts with a brawl between two non-kin males, often about women, sometimes about accusations of theft, insults or infringement on privacy. As we have said, the Kapsiki are quick to take offense from "strangers" *(muntibu,* people from other villages) as well as from fellow-villagers, so an inducement is not hard to find. Many a fight starts at the market, after the men have over-indulged in beer and discussions grow heated. When two men come to blows, the type of battle depends on their relationship. If they are members of different clans, both clans may join battle or their respective wards may join in, depending on the men present. If men of both wards happen to be present, a fight between both wards may follow, but more often both clans fight corporately. In battles within the village, kinship relations dominate territorial relations; in intervillage war the reverse is true.

Whenever the two clashing clans belong to opposite phratries, the whole phratry joins in the battle; in most instances this is the case and most *mpa derha* are fights between the village's halves. In fact the main function of the phratries is just this division in war. When people narrate the conflicts of the past, this is the type they remember. The other members see the men fighting, grab their weapons and the *mpa derha* is under way. Most men do not have even the slightest hunch what the whole thing is about, but that does not detract from the fun. As one *ngacE* clan informant stated:

> Several times I joined the *mpa derha* against the *makwiyE* (opposite phratry). I never knew the reason the fight occurred. The last time it occurred during a funeral dance; all at once I saw my brothers fighting, so I charged too. Those things often happened. Most of the times nobody was killed, as no one will ever use arrows inside Mogodé.

Burial dances are other classic occasions for starting an internal fight. Often people resent their bereavement and wish to heap guilt for the untimely departure on other people, throwing insults and accusations at each other. As people always dance with weapons, a *mpa derha* easily follows. Disputes over women are a frequent cause of war. As we shall discuss at length in the next chapter, two consecutive husbands of the same woman are enemies by definition. Battle is at hand when they meet. They should not belong to the same village, but if they do, the relationship may be disturbed for years:

> One of the last *mpa derha* in Mogodé originated about ten years ago from a conflict between the *makwiyE* and *makwajE* clans. One of the latter had "stolen" a wife from a *makwiyE* and his transgression resulted in a *mpa derha*. The fight between the two husbands broke out during a burial dance and quickly escalated to a full day's fighting between the two village halves. At the end of the day one *makwiyE* was slain. Now, ten years later, the relations between the two clans are still strained; few *makwiyE* men have close *makwajE* friends and no *makwiyE* father likes to give his daughter to a man of the enemy clan, as this death has been neither avenged nor paid for.

This latter example brings up the matter of settlement. Fighting between clan members is settled by other clan members but fighting between clans or phratries can only be moderated by those persons personifying the village as a whole, either the village headman or the officiator in sacrifice. The first is the most likely to intervene. Assisted by his friend, the *tlewefe*, and some ward headmen, he tries to separate the fighting parties, shouting and pleading, often in vain. When Kapsiki are fighting, they dislike interference even more than usual, so many battles are terminated by the falling dusk and not by the efforts of village functionaries.

The death of a warrior is another way of ending hostilities. As the above mentioned case indicates, people do get killed, even though the weaponry is aimed at wounding more than killing. Death within a village is a very serious matter, a severe rupture in the social relations, which has to be restored in one way or another. This restoration normally takes the form of payment of *keluhu,* blood money. After a death the village chief and his assistants succeed in calming the fighting parties mainly because people are shocked by the actual brutality of death and curious as to its details. The slain man is taken to his compound, and burial preparations begin. Sons or brothers tour the villages spreading news of the death as related people in other villages will attend the last day of the burial dances.

The mother's brother of the deceased is informed specifically; he has the main responsibility of negotiating a death payment. If he lives in the same village he will do so directly. After the burial he gathers some close patrilineal relatives to help him visit the village and the compounds of the patrilineal kin of the culprit. In these *rhE* they amass all objects of wealth they can find such as gowns, spears and ornaments. They fill baskets with sorghum and corn and have their women carry them away. They then go into the fields where the mother's brother confiscates sheep and goats. If he can find the cattle of the debtors, he will take some of them away. Thus blood money is not paid but is taken. The mother's brother decides the amount and simply stops the plunder when he deems the payment sufficient. No one can resist him, no one would dare, for "a death is never fully paid." The main judicial instrument in Kapsiki culture, a magico-religious means that regulates all debt relations, is especially potent in these cases: "It follows blood." After confiscation, the mother's brother divides the amassed wealth between the clan of his slain sister's son and his own patrilineal kin. This way of "paying *keluhu*" presents a continuing threat for all valuable property such as cattle.

Any Kapsiki can be taxed to pay for the actions of an aggressive clan brother. For this reason most cattle are herded by non-kin friends, Mbororo Fulani, for instance. In case of homicide, the mother's brothers of the victim cannot take cattle from the herd of a non-related man. Moreover, no one but the actual owner and his friend know to whom the cattle actually belong; even their children may not be fully informed. Thus, property may be safeguarded from the transgressions of brothers.

The total amount of the *keluhu* depends on several factors; the size and wealth of the accountable group are the most important. The *keluhu* is taken from the whole clan in the case of a clan-fight, from the phratry when the two village halves have been warring, or in some cases from a whole village. The latter instance deserves some explanation:

> In a fight between men from Garta and Mogodé, one Garta warrior was killed. The mother's brother of the dead man, assisted by some of his classificatory daughter's sons who lived in Mogodé, came up to Mogodé village to take the *keluhu*. Together they took four cows, twenty goats, a dozen blankets, a huge heap of ornaments and a forest of spears. Other people from Garta who came along with him carried all these belongings to Garta, after which the mother's brother announced the debt had been settled. All Mogodé clans were taxed about equally and no one could prohibit the Garta plunder of his riches.

This fight, too, is called a *mpa derha*, but it is a borderline case. Although we have said that villages are autarchic politically and socially, some bonds between villages may exist. One of these is a tradition of common origin between clusters of two or three villages. Each village acknowledges some "brother" settlements, often situated at some distance, which originate from the same ancestral migration. The founders may have been brothers or may stand in a father-son relationship. For Mogodé the villages of Garta and Rhumshi (Mbororo) are thus kin. No war parties are ever organized against them, and occasional manslaughter, as shown above, can be settled by *keluhu*. However, this is rare, as the distance between the villages renders contact between the inhabitants rare. In these cases payment of *keluhu* is a more delicate affair than within the village, but it can be done with great circumspection on the part of the mother's brother, who should take care lest too great a plunder would cause a new homicide. Besides, Kapsiki like to boast about their ability to pay a huge *keluhu*, as well as about war exploits and heroic deeds, a tendency towards conspicuous giving that manifests itself in several other ways; i.e., in marriage proceedings.

The fighting rules between related villages vary somewhat from one village cluster to another; some villages in the south of the Kapsiki territory that are bound together by a tradition of common origin still do fight each other in formal battles. Their relationship is reflected in the fact that they do not capture slaves from one another, thus removing one important inducement for fighting.

Full-scale war, in which all available weaponry is used, occurred between unrelated villages. Our opening chapter was an example of such warfare. Fighting between villages continued until the 1950's, when war was stopped. Two orders of battle were distinguished—the battle fought on the *rhwa mpa,* battleplace, in which the whole village participated, and the *rhwebe*, the raid. Both types of conflict involved the use of bows and poisoned arrows, weapons that aim at killing, not wounding the adversary. The war of our opening chapter was a *mpa te mpa*, "true war." Raids were often conducted after a war to avenge a killing or to capture slaves. Aiming at revenge, a small party of young men would sneak into enemy territory and hide on the outskirts of the village. When at dawn the unsuspecting men and

Mock battle is part of the boys' initiation.

women emerged from their huts to fetch water or to start for their fields, they were attacked and captured. If slaves were not sought but simply revenge, one might sneak into the enemy village after nightfall and shoot at people gathered around the fire. An example of such a raid can be found in the attack by the people of Kortchi on the village of Gawar mentioned previously.

When avenging a death, the men were not interested in finding the enemy warrior responsible for the killing; they wanted a life for a life, despite the fact that everyone was well aware of who did the initial killing. In the *mpa te mpa* everyone knew who delivered the fatal blow or shot. After a successsul raid, the raiding party, when at a safe distance from the enemy village, would shout the name of the valiant warrior responsible for the killing. The mourning enemies would thus know what *katsala* (warrior) adversary claimed the death. Nevertheless, a counterraid would not seek to avenge the death by slaying the culprit.

Corpses were always left on the battlefield to be retrieved by the family and village members of the slain. In actual battles, there was no need to be concerned about carrying corpses away; people were wounded or killed on the skirmish line surrounded by kinsmen. In a raid or when captured, enemies often were killed, and the corpses were left behind for the enemy kinsmen to bury. However, the genitals of the men were cut and taken in triumph toward the killers' villages, to be thrown to the old men and kept by *mnzefE*, the ritual officiant of the *ngacE* clan, who acted as a ritual war leader. No direct mediation was possible during battles — they were fought out, not talked out. After a battle, if contact was needed between the enemy villages to negotiate the ransom of a captured enemy, there was no overall authority to settle the matter. The immunity of the *wuzemakwa* (literally "daughter's son"), a young boy whose mother originally came from the enemy village, was employed. He was sent to the village as an emissary; no one would kill a daughter's son.

Slaves were formerly the spoils of war. Any enemy man, woman or child could become a slave and the use of non-lethal weapons in battle (such as iron and wooden clubs) was aimed at capturing enemies alive. In raids or in pursuit of a fleeing enemy, the chances were high to capture or to be captured. *Katsala* men not only were valiant warriors, but they were the quickest runners too. Their swiftness was important in two ways. They were the most likely ones to capture enemies running towards their home village and they themselves were very difficult to overtake in pursuit. Any enemy captured was immediately considered a slave. While women and children were taken toward the village without much ado, a captured man called for rejoicing and humiliation of the enemy. An armed man could normally only be taken alive if he surrendered; he would throw his weapons to the ground and shout, "Do not kill me" when he saw that his chances were nil. His captors collected his weapons and returned in a triumphant procession to their village. The captured slave was forced to sing derisive songs about his own village, praising the valor of his captors and exhorting his fellows and kinsmen to come and be a slave too, "as no one can equal the strength of their enemies." The warriors of the winning party sang special songs, *geza,* blew antelope and buffalo horns and returned to their village singing, shouting and dancing with the weapons of their captive. *MnzefE* was waiting for them in his compound. He received the captured weapons, broke the bow of the slave and put all these treasures of triumph underneath his granary, an important place of sanctuary. The slave was chained or immobilized by putting his leg in a hollow log while his captors forced him to wear women's clothes. He would either be sold to slave dealers or ransomed by his kinsmen. The latter procedure was the most common. Only captives with few or poor kinsmen could not afford one or two cows. Although captors gained double when selling to external dealers (Fulani, Hausa merchants), they preferred their captives to be bought back by their village.

Revenge and slaves may be the goal of a war, but the original motive often was quite another matter. Inducement to conflict, as we have seen, stemmed from other sources. When asked, informants state that a war could break out on any pretext. "Why should there have to be a reason? Are they not our enemies?" Grief through bereavement accounted for a number of conflicts. During a funeral rite the young men of the village gathered some special herbs and plants from the bush, and in the case of an untimely death they penetrated deep into enemy territory in their search, in order to provoke war. Even today, when battles can no longer be fought, they still provoke quarrels. A survey of reasons for fighting, internal as well as external, shows some more endemic problems contributing to the outbreak of battle.

Table 4: Reasons for Fighting

	external conflicts	conflicts within the village
theft	9	2
women	9	6
quarrels at beer parties	2	5
ritual	6	4
surprise attack	2	2
	28	19

Under "ritual" several causes are counted: burial rites, the showing off of young boys during initiation time and the transgression of hunting rights during ceremonial hunts. Together they accounted for a significant number of wars between villages. Still, theft is more important in this respect. Kapsiki emphatically state that in former times theft was all too common ("We grew up with theft"), but since pacification its incidence has diminished. We shall dwell on this problem later, in Chapter Six. In any case, theft of goats, cows, sweet potatoes, etc., easily rouses the emotions.

Conflicts over women constitute the largest single cause of war inside the village as well as between non-kin villages. We gave one example of this in our opening case; we will dwell on the strains generated by the marriage system later. The quarrels at beer parties also account for quite a few incidents within the village, again centering around women.

This endemic warfare has had far-reaching consequences within the fabric of Kapsiki social life, both for the relations between villages and for the social and matrimonial systems within villages. Communication between villages evidently suffered from the threat of war; the fact that markets were only installed after pacification by the Europeans underscores the economic importance of this fact. Informal contacts between members of different villages have been scarce and were obviously not facilitated by the threat of slave raiding. Nevertheless, fighting did cement a bond between and within villages. We have described the Kapsiki village as a loose conglomerate of independent compounds. Even though lineage and clan membership do furnish a social grid for individual action, these groups show few corporate characteristics and cannot effectively counterbalance individual autarky. In armed conflicts, however, unity was stressed; it was in battle that the clan could "show its strength," rallying behind the aggrieved member to fight the other clan. The bonding was even greater for the phratries; these village halves could only be analyzed with respect to intravillage fighting. Villages as a whole emerge as a relevant social unit in intervillage warfare. Traditions of common origin that slumber throughout peacetime suddenly come alive, uniting and dividing warparties and dictating compensation for manslaughter. The ritual complementarity of the various clans within the village clearly shows itself in war. The blacksmiths, who in normal times are marginal members of Kapsiki social life, perform a vital role as they furnish weapons and poison. Even if warfare precludes the formation and organization of a political unity beyond the village community, it enhances the unity and sense of group membership of the lower-level units. A sense of unity prevailed in fighting. People did not fight strangers, they fought fellows they knew by name who might be allied by some marriage tie. Once in another Mogodé-Sirakouti war, five people from Sirakouti had been killed. During their burial, the Mogodé village mourned too: five was too many.

War unites in several other ways, too. It is a regulated system; the rules of weapon escalation (see Table 3) are among the most generally shared social norms and values. In contrast to variation in culture between villages, the war system stands out as a uniform, shared set of rules, followed by all

Kapsiki and Higi. Infringement of conflict rules are very scarce. We have not been able to find examples of unjust use of weapons. Even the *mpa te mpa,* war between villages is regulated with its special battlefield, fixed weaponry and the general norm that victory should be attained by cunning, swiftness and the agility of the individual warriors. One could easily conceive of several strategies to kill enemies or capture slaves, such as striking at the back, development of mobile shelters, surprise attacks at the flanks, or the development of new weapons. None of those possibilities are used. In our opinion this stems from the fact that fighting is not truly to capture slaves, to take revenge, nor a natural consequence of disputes over women or property; people fight because it is the most accepted thing to do. It is the evident means to prove oneself, to stand out among the comrades and age mates. In short, it is a means of self-realization. Wars are fought when agriculture allows; i.e., in the dry season. They should be considered a diversion. In previous times, war was an actual diversion; now it serves as a shared verbal-oral diversion. People recount with great enthusiasm their past heroic deeds. As an example of this attitude here is a short monologue from one of the oldest men in Mogodé:

> I never expected to grow so old. Did I not make war so that I should not have to become so decrepit? I have been shot at at least 19 times in my lifetime but the arrows never entered my flesh. A real good *rhwE* (protective magic) protects me and my sons' children will have it. I found it in the field. (A standard expression meaning he killed an enemy for it. His clan, the *ngacE* know this *rhwE* very well and consider it their most potent shield.) The Fulani shot at me often too, but I killed several of them. Nowadays I am a walking corpse; what use am I? But formerly, yes, in the old days I was a famous fighter, a real *katsala.* If my brother Zera and I did not join the war, there would be no fighting. I fought all villages around Mogodé, except Garta. The was is good; yes, fighting is good. I gained some slaves too and I was never captured myself. Yes, I recollect capturing *Kweji Blama* from Sir, and once I assisted in the capture of three men from Wula. Those three have been paid by the Wula people with one bull, and *Kweji Mblama* returned to Sir, after his people paid a cow, six goats and two gowns. Ah yes, I love to fight. When the big war against the Fulani came about I happened to be very ill, and I cried and cried as I had to stay at home.

On the whole, the unifying function of conflict bears some dialectical features. War unites people by providing division on a lower level. The ties it creates between individuals originate from the possibility for showmanship. This very same dialectical relationship between harmony and conflict will be shown in the next chapter.

In this chapter we have described the socio-territorial system of the

Kapsiki with its system of internal wars. Among the other tribes of these Mandara mountains similar systems may be found. Patrilineal clans with virilocal marriage is a general feature (as it is in most of savannah Africa). Kapsiki villages are slightly larger than those of their neighbors. The chief's position is stronger in most other tribes; the Kapsiki are more egalitarian than most. War has been endemic among the other tribes too, as it has been in most of West Africa before colonization. The impact of colonial peace and the halt of slave raiding and trading can hardly be overestimated in Africa.

Thus, this social system of the Kapsiki may be taken as more or less representative of all isolated tribes who fought off slave raiders while on the fringe of a larger former emirate.

The peculiarities of Kapsiki culture emerge in the next three chapters. In religion, intercultural variation is large. The Kapsiki marriage system is not unique but it has some specific features not found in most neighboring tribes.

4

Religion

Tribal religions are among the most elusive topics to study. Yet, no traditional culture can be understood without some knowledge of beliefs, rituals and festivals. This is certainly true for the Kapsiki. This chapter presents an overview of the main points of Kapsiki religion, including belief, sacrifice and communal ritual. Kapsiki belief is quite individualistic; their principal notion of a supernatural being could be dubbed "a personal God." Based on the belief in an intimate relation between this world and the supernatural one, a number of rituals are performed frequently guided by divination.

In fact, the term "supernatural," used here as a general term for "matters of belief," is not very appropriate in the Kapsiki case. "The other side of this world" would be a better term; like the two sides of a sheet of paper belong together, the other side belongs to this world.

Divination is the most direct way of communicating with this world. Sacrifice is the common act which relates both sides of one's existence to each other. In both divination and sacrifice, the main topic of this book — relations between men and women — can be traced.

Kapsiki religion does unite a village at certain times. The communal rites are important in this. Governed by agricultural rhythm, burial, initiation and marriage engender a series of festive rites important to the Kapsiki. These three ceremonies are equally important to us in order to understand Kapsiki life. The short overview presented shows how these rituals aim at a yearly "harvest of people," among which the new brides and wives figure prominently.

In a traditional religion, the tension and stress of social life are transformed into a code of action and belief. Solutions to the most enduring and endemic problems are offered. Religious processes are of a very dialectical nature: stressing problems on the one hand while simultaneously denying the existence of any tension at all. In Kapsiki religion, conflicts between norms and reality, as well as between the usual individualism versus pure collective harmony are found.

The Other Side of the World

A household head finds substantiation for his cherished autonomy in the religious complex of sacrifices, divination, initiation rites, myth and magic. Of prime importance is the Kapsiki belief in *shala*—god or God. *Shala* is a key concept; *a shala menete*, "God has done it," is often heard in conversations. The meaning is that things have taken a bad turn, but no matter, things are what they are. *Shala* has quickly been taken to represent the Christian God by missionaries, but it is more complicated than that. Each person has his own *shala*, his or her personal god. Each social unit—say clan, ward, village as well as mountain, river or forested waterside—has its *shala*. Inside the family the father has his *shala* and so does each of his wives and children. When asked about these many *shala* the Kapsiki state that, in essence, they are not different, but one and the same. In daily speech one never indicates which *shala* is meant, as the context makes it sufficiently clear. A man sacrificing for himself addresses his own personal *shala* but when all household members are present the *shala ta rhE* (house god) is implied. In the village sacrifice the god of the whole village is sought after. In the ultimate extension, *shala pelE rhweme* can be used if one wants to stress the one God in heaven in which all individual *shala* unite:

> Though the concept of *shala* may be analytically vague, *shala* neverthe- less is a reality for Kapsiki. *Shala* exists as everyone can readily see. The following statement by *Vandu Tsehe* at a ward sacrifice is significant: "Nobody can say that he or she does not know *shala*. *Shala* made every- thing. We cultivate the sorghum and *shala* provides rain. There is no man who does not know *shala*. We are here because *shala* wants us here."

Things become even more complicated when animals are considered to have their own *shala*; even some special places are called *shala*. In that instance, the place *shala* has its own *shala* again, *shala ta shala*. All *shala* are in heaven, a place just like here, doing things as people do. They are in fact also called *mbeli pelE rhweme,* or "people up high." They are followed closely in word and action, our world being a carbon copy of theirs. Dliyeda, an old neighbor, tried to explain the intricacies of the supernatural world to me:

> My *shala* and yours are doing just like us, sitting together in the shade
> of a tree. If they sit down, we sit down too; should they stand up, up we
> go. We are the slaves of *shala*. Should my *shala* steal, I steal. If he enters
> war, I do too. A mistake by my *shala* means my mistake. If he is rich I
> become wealthy; if he is a courageous hunter my game will be plentiful;
> if he is hurt, I feel the pain; and once he dies I am done for.

In this world we are the slaves of *shala* (another informant conjured the
image of a horse ridden by his *shala*); we are their dead ones too. A
deceased *shala* descends from heaven and stays on the rubbish heap waiting
to enter an open womb after sexual intercourse and become a fetus—a new
Kapsiki-to-be. Upon entering, the woman becomes pregnant. The Kapsiki
call a fetus *shala,* but someone in heaven will assume duties as the personal
shala counting the months of pregnancy and after nine moons opening the
womb.

The heavenly population of *shala* has its own higher order of *shala* and,
in theory, the process repeats itself endlessly. In everyday life only one's
own *shala* is of any importance. In the same way we, the living, are the *shala*
of those beneath us. In other words, we are the gods of the people who died
before us. *Dliyeda* again:

> We are the *shala* of the dead people. When I die, my shadow descends
> and enters into a woman's womb, becoming a child again down below.
> They live just like we do, the same villages, the same sorcerers, and may
> be even stronger. If these from below die, their shadow descends even
> further and they become the *shala* of the people beneath them.

So Kapsiki cosmology presents a fascinating cascade of ever more spirits
descending one stage per generation. The beginning is not known; neither is
the end. In fact, the question of ultimate origin is not posed. Our informant
Dliyeda, when pushed towards an answer to that un-Kapsiki-like question,
sighed "Where is yesterday's wind?" Another point is that the concept of
the "supernatural" is not very relevant for the Kapsiki. The notion of the
other side of the world portrays the Kapsiki views much better.

One should note throughout that the notion of a cosmological *system* is
foreign to the Kapsiki. No one ever presents a total view nor a coherent
theology. In speaking with us, no one *systematized* the Kapsiki cosmology
stating, for example, that at death, *shala* dies, his respondent in the
nether world dies too, thus resulting in an infinite column of living beings
descending stages as disembodied spirits. Kapsiki are only intensely
interested in their own direct *shala* and somewhat less interested in the
"people in the ground." Theology ends there. Differences of opinion on
these matters are common and present no problem at all. If one Kapsiki
states that all his own faults are due to the *shala* who makes him sin, his beer
companion corrects him saying, "Everybody is responsible for his own

faults; we are the horse *shala* rides on, and a horse that throws its master is at fault.''

Religion is lived, not speculated upon. Whatever cosmology one may adopt, it is the relationship not the theology which counts. Feelings of dependency on and resignation to *shala* abound. After the death of a child, a miscarriage, a bad harvest or the disappearance of a wife, Kapsiki simply sigh and say *"shala menete, tsarha nza"* (God did it, such is life). In

A blacksmith drummer greets the *shala* of the compound.

principle, *shala* aims at the well-being of his living manifestation, but some ambivalence is discernible. *Shala* may punish too and many a misfortune is attributed to *shala*: surely some taboo must have been broken, some mistakes must have been made and *shala* has taken appropriate action. The culprit is "out-of-harmony" *(ndegema)* with his *shala*. Two courses of action are open. One is very dignified: "look with the eyes"; i.e., suffer in tranquility, just bear the burden, suffer one's fate and live with it. A Kapsiki is considered very mature and grown-up, "looking just with his eyes." Men emphatically state that women tend to follow the second course: that of action, "Because they are like children; they cannot bear their sorrow." This active course, in reality by no means restricted to women, encompasses divination and sacrifice, which together form the core of Kapsiki ritual.

Taboo regulations are numerous and the willing or unknowing infraction of one of them is only to be expected. They range from whistling in a millet field, entering a compound where a sacrifice is being performed, killing a pregnant goat, cutting firewood on a sacred place, to having one's rooster crow on top of the granary. If none of these taboos has been broken, the erring person has probably taken an oath somewhere and broken it. *Shala* punishes oathbreakers. The Kapsiki happen to be consummate oathtakers, swearing frequently to convince fellow men or women, "If this is not true, let the thunderbolt hit me, let the epidemic kill me, let *shala* take me."

One's own *shala* may be dangerous, but the God of other people is even more harmful. Even between close kin the ambivalence of *shala* is clear:

> At the burial rites of *TizhE Kwebe*, one of his six daughters was absent. She did not dare to come. After many miscarriages, she had at last given birth to a child, and in divination she had been told that she should never return to her father's house because the *shala* of his compound would kill her child.

Divination

Any problem, just as any important decision, calls for divination. In Chapter Two, we described the techniques used by the blacksmiths. Here we shall focus on the social processes involved in ascertaining the views of the supernatural world. When an individual Kapsiki addresses the "other side of this world" in divination, the main foci and points of interest in the culture are apparent. Divination is a mirror for society; individuals project their own situation in order to read back their overt and secret wishes, their frustrations and ambiguities, their secure beliefs and firm values.

The main problems for a man in Kapsiki society center around the stability of his compound: the women he has married, the children they will bear, his harvest, and his relations with his kinsmen. A Kapsiki woman is concerned about her health and that of her children, infertility and infant death, her relations with co-wives and other members of her husband's village. Both parties independently consult the diviner and try to keep their partner from knowing too much. Even the blacksmiths, whose marriages show more unity, follow the pattern:

> *Kweji,* wife of one of his fellow blacksmiths, consults the crab at *Cewuve's* compound. Her husband, *Teri,* is a diviner too, but of course no woman would dream of consulting her own husband, as "one can never tell one's husband everything." Here at *Cewuve's* she withholds information as well. *Kweji* tells the diviner that she wants to take some clothes to her married daughter who now lives in a faraway village, but her husband does not agree. How should she get the clothes to her daughter? The crab completely ignores her question and puts her on the spot: "Why do you want to run away from your husband?" *Kweji* denies this, and the crab foretells illness or death. "Someone will come to your door with bad news; you will cry over it." *Kweji:* "That must be my daughter!" Is it her mother-in-law who has cursed her? The diviner assures her that *shala* has done all this and tells her what she has to sacrifice in order to evade the bad news. The crab has spoken. At that moment *Teri,* her husband, joins them. He is a chance visitor to *Cewuve's* compound; he did not know his wife was consulting a diviner. *Cewuve* gives him a strong lecture on how to treat his wife lest she run away. *Teri:* "This wife is one of those that runs around. She will not stay; she just came here to have a child, and if she has another one, she will walk even in full daylight to the next guy." He leaves in anger, after which *Kweji* explains to *Cewuve:* "That is not true. I did not come only to have a child. A few weeks ago *Teri's* brother consulted the crab for me, and it indicated that *Teri's* mother has cursed me. *Teri* should give her some meat and a chicken in order to have her remove that curse. *Teri* does not want to do that, and now I want to be sure if my mother-in-law cursed me or not." *Cewuve:* "No, she did not. Just take some millet from this ward and from your own, mix it with dregs of red and white beer, and leave this mixture for one night outside your hut door. Early next morning call in *Teri's* children to assist you, put the stuff on your (sacrificial) jar and ask *shala* for a baby. The rest of the mixture you drop on the road outside your compound." *Kweji,* after discussing some further details of the sacrifice, leaves for her home and performs the sacrifice the next morning.
>
> After about a year she became pregnant, but left her husband anyway.

This example shows how man and wife use divination to know about each other's motives. Wives considering running away—the main subject of our next chapter—assess their chances in the present or proposed village, keeping the information strictly to themselves. Many a husband asks the crab why his wife has not become pregnant, as infertility is a prime reason for departure. His sacrifice aims at keeping his wife in his compound. The mechanism of divination, however, allows for quite some leeway in interpretation on the part of the diviner. The dozen different strips of calabash lying higgledy-piggledy on the wet sand give only very general clues and answers, so the diviner has to fill in the rest himself. In the above example, *Cewuve* knew his client very well and reacted accordingly. Without the visit of her husband, however, he would not have known her true motive. Even so, the wife went home, taking her secrets with her. This is a very common practice: a client tries to keep the relevant problems secret. The blacksmith-diviner, quick-witted and sharp as blacksmiths reputedly are, should not know too much. The crab should answer, not the diviner. Many clients put the straws representing their situation and problems into the pot with their own hands. No blacksmith is to be trusted entirely, because no other person should have too large an influence in one's private life. Although the divination system calls for an informed intermediary, the Kapsiki try to keep it as private as possible. As diviners are men, Kapsiki women never state their intention of running away, but use any sort of ruse to keep the diviner from knowing. *Kweji* used such a ruse in vain, but many other women consult diviners who know less about them. They might choose a blacksmith from another village, perhaps their village of birth.

Ideally one should build up a lasting relationship with a diviner; permanence is usually based on correct predictions. If a diviner is proved wrong, one simply looks for another. If he is right, there is no reason to change.

Diviners have, therefore, to work with a minimum amount of information, foretelling things that have to be right. They are helped by two particular aspects of Kapsiki culture: the general style of conversation and the Kapsiki attitude toward misfortune. Kapsiki tend to converse in parables and hyperboles, often using many obscure expressions and comparisons. The real *rhena za* (men's talk) is very cryptic and smiths make full use of it to convey an ambivalent message. In the example above, the prediction, "you will receive news which will make you cry," could be applied to a great many situations. The actual words used for the prediction were even more cryptic: "The morning will wet your eyes."

Predicting misfortune is the most important work of a diviner. Kapsiki say, "Misfortune is the real reality." A client of *Cewuve* once said: "I always consult *Cewuve* because he predicts misfortune, so I know what is really going to happen." Mishaps are the fabric of life and if one just lets things happen, misfortune will be one's lot. The world is not to be trusted. In any case, from the diviner's perspective, predicting evil reduces the problem of being proven wrong. If no misfortune befalls his client despite being foretold, who will complain? If sacrifices do not help, it is always

Blacksmith Cewuve clarifies the predictions the crabfish has offered for his client, Zra Dabala.

possible that they were not performed properly, or their effect might have been lessened by new complications. For a diviner who foretells misfortune, there is no problem in explaining away discrepancies! On the other hand, explaining why someone who was pronounced safe happens to be knee-deep in trouble is far more difficult indeed.

Sacrifice

After divination the problems are clear and the client has specific instructions on how to appease the other world through sacrifice. Performing a sacrifice, either for oneself, for a compound, a ward, a lineage or the whole village, is the core of Kapsiki ritual. All sacrifices can be indicated with the same word *melE*, meaning "a place to speak about health," and health is just what is spoken about:

> Let us be healthy, let sickness pass, please God send the illnesses to our neighbors. Let the bad things go by without attacking us: if someone is to be attacked, please pick another person.

The crab may often indicate a very small offering, a spoonful of beer dregs, a few grains of cooked millet, a piece of millet mush, or peanut paste; these instructions are followed immediately:

> *Zera Mpa,* having consulted the crab over his second wife's infertility, promptly follows its counsel. All *Zera's* wives ask for a handful of millet from the village chief, and they bury it in a piece of cloth for one night before their doorstep. Next morning they mix the grains with some sand, grind it, and mix it with beer dreg and a few peanuts. Each wife takes her white sacrificial stone from the deep recesses of her hut; all three wives put the sticky paste on their *melE,* at the same moment saying *kelEngelEng* (health).

This is daily, standard practice. The "real" thing however is the sacrifice of an animal on the main *melE*—a sacrificial jar representing the deceased father or mother of the compound head, which serves as an intermediary to *shala*. This is the sacrifice for the whole compound, to solve problems of the nuclear family such as sterility, death or absentee women. In the following example *Sunu TerimcE,* whose only wife has not borne a child for more than five years, follows the indication of the crab and holds a *melE rhE,* a home sacrifice:

> Early in the morning before sunrise, *Sunu* selects a red rooster from his wife's brood, and puts a wooden board in his house entrance to keep

anyone from intruding inadvertently. Having tied up the little rooster, he mixes some flour and water in a calabash and reaches for his *melE,* a 10 liter jar with a narrow opening which he keeps under one of his granaries. Having set the *melE* against his compound wall, he takes the cow horn from the opening, and pours some of his millet cream into it saying, "Father, give me health." A mouthful of cream is spit over his breast and belly, "Take the evil things from my belly; make me healthy, I say. I want to hear the bad news from outside, not from inside. Whoever is jealous, I will crush under my heels." The rest of the cream is poured on the wall: "Here, eat your things, leave!" and by now the "evil things" are expected to leave the compound. For the second phase of the sacrifice *Sunu* takes his rooster, plucks the feathers from its throat and adorns the jar with them. His five-year-old son, *TizhE,* joins him and takes the rooster's head firmly in his little hand. God should give a boy like him again, so it is more than appropriate that he should be in it. *Sunu* cuts the rooster's throat so that the first drops of blood fall on the jar, and smears the jar with the dying rooster's blood: "Here my God, here is something to eat." Dumping the carcass on the ground he watches the fowl beat its wings, and gratefully observes "thank you, God, thank you" (the beating of wings is a sign of acceptance by *shala*).

Just after the killing, *KwafashE,* who has been looking from her doorstep, runs towards the jar, gets some blood and cream from her husband and pours it on her (deceased mother's) little jar, saying, "my God, give me a child; take the evil things from my belly; let someone else be barren."

In the evening the rooster is cooked with the rest of the meal, and the ritual is terminated. *Sunu* twice puts a little bit of its liver and a morsel of millet mush on the jar, which has been put back under the granary, saying, "Here is your food, father. Give us health; give us children; take away sterility; take away the evil things."

Finally, man, wife and only son eat the rest of the chicken and the mush. Outsiders are excluded throughout the ritual and the whole thing is strictly private, although a neighbor would know that a sacrifice is being performed. Afterwards, in beer parties or in repose at the ward meeting place, the sacrifice is freely spoken about and no secrecy prevails. However, should someone enter the compound during the sacrifice both the sacrifice and the intruder would be, as the Kapsiki say, spoiled, *bezemte.* A new sacrifice and a consultation of the crab by the hapless visitor would be called for.

Should a wife stay barren or should the next infant die, more drastic measures are called for. The same sort of sacrifice can be repeated on a larger scale, often including a goat sacrifice. The nuclear family no longer suffices. This type of sacrifice draws a much larger circle of kinsmen, neighbors and friends into the proceedings. The sacrifice follows roughly the same pattern, the main difference being that a lot of red beer is brewed before the actual date to be served as a libation on the *melE*. The day after the ritual, the rest of the beer (by far the largest part) is consumed by a crowd of invited or semi-invited kinsmen, neighbors and friends. This *tE melE* (sacrificial beer) is one of the highlights in the Kapsiki social life. Not only do the Kapsiki love to drink beer, but they also revel in speaking wise words at these public meetings. Following the order of age and importance, all old men drink and speak up, thank the host for his generosity, and admonish all present to follow their illustrious example, all the while downing the beer with astonishing speed. The village chief, always present, offers lengthy and intricately worded advice which is applauded by everyone and followed by almost no one. Drinking and speaking last the whole morning; at the end the 100-odd liters of beer are exhausted. During these proceedings, the family stays inside the compound. The wife in question never shows her face to the visitors.

If infertility still prevails after all this effort, the whole performance might be repeated with a blacksmith officiating in the sacrifice (although this could have happened in the first instance also). Usually, more direct methods are called for. The sacrifice of a goat is performed on *shala* place which is both more sacred and more dangerous. Early in the morning a blacksmith leaves the village with the barren woman and one of her husband's goats. Way out in the bush, in the place where the spirits roam, the smith kills the animal and leaves it for the spirits. Sometimes he simply breaks its legs. This sacrifice is not eaten; it is one of the strongest measures a woman can take.

It is not, however, the last resort. The indigenous pharmacopia is filled with medicines and magical means to enhance fertility and health. It is called *rhwE* by the Kapsiki and as such is mainly dispersed by blacksmiths. The same holds for the men's continual problem of vanishing wives. A man might use sacrifice in order to have a woman stay in his compound and/or he might resort to magic. Expensive and slightly dangerous as it may be, magic is perceived as a real help when troubles engulf the hapless individual. Magical means to secure either women or children range from the simple *hwEbE* (a special onion sold by the blacksmith) to a complicated series of very secret precepts for which one pays a sorcerer dearly:

> A man who wants to marry many women plants a *keyitu* plant (Grewia) in his house, collects its fruits, adds some grains of wild couch and hides these in the little head pad the woman wears for bearing loads. The pad is well greased with peanut oil and stacked away in a pot. Whenever a woman comes to the village to find a husband, he rubs the grains, some dirt from the pad and some perfume bought at the market, on his hands. When he flicks his fingers to hers (part of the acquaintance procedure),

she will follow him immediately and never long for another man. However, she will certainly leave him unless he performs another rite, in which a stone used at the market place is put on her sleeping mat when she is asleep. This will not solve all problems; jealousy might enter the compound. To chase envy, the husband buries Ficus flowers and Boswellia fruits on three spots in and near the wife's hut. Now new problems may enter. Infertility might be one of them, and a score of rites address this problem. After all these precautions one can be sure that the children born to the magically wed woman will cling to their parent's home. In order to have his daughter leave the compound in marriage, a special chicken sacrifice is called for. The slaughter of a goat is required at the initiation of a boy to have him settle. Only after all these measures can a man expect to have a normal married life.

Communal Ritual

In the course of the annual cycle, a series of communal rites are held in which the main "rites de passage" are integrated. The smaller segment of these rites are agricultural ones such as the rain ritual, rites protecting the crops against vermin and disease, and the numerous prescriptions and proscriptions accompanying harvest and grain storage. The main Kapsiki concern however is with people: how to get and keep the house full of people. The yearly agricultural cycle dominates social and ritual life, and most "rites de passage," such as marriage, initiation and second burial have a fixed place on the ritual calendar. Following Kapsiki logic, the cycle starts with the second burial of all people buried the year before. In about February, the chief blacksmith of the village performs the final rites on the tombs of all recently dead, each on its separate day assisted by a handful of the dead people's nearest kinsmen. The focal point of these proceedings is the dedication of the sacrificial jar, on which the sons and daughters will perform their individual and compound offerings. Addressing their father or mother through this jar, invoking them to beg *shala* on their behalf, they easily identify the jar with "their father's head." In the burial ritual a mixture of beer and millet is poured on the tomb, the late parent's sacrificial jar is broken by the blacksmith, and the new jar is carried home adorned with exactly the same symbols that the corpse has been decorated with during the funeral dances.

After February the last season of the year is thus truly ended and the new harvest can be expected, a harvest of people rather than of grains. The shadows of the dead, weird and dangerous in their envy of the living, no longer roam the fields around the village. They are now on their way down to the next stage, a shadowy life below the surface of the earth. The next thing to do concerns marriage. All girls coming of age in that year will marry their first (but not last!) husband in the next lunar month. For the village this implies a continuous series of eating and drinking bouts. Huge wedding parties are held in which the clans of both groom and bride are joined by the elders of the ward in a ritual and feast, demarcating the transition of the bride from her parent's compound to her husband's. The girl is brought to her new compound with considerable care. In the blessings given to her some of the inherent Kapsiki contradictions reappear: the bride's people extoll their own gift and warn the girl to stay at her husband's, while at the same time hinting to the bride that she might be given to another man after the brideprice has been "repaid" in children. In the next chapter we shall follow a typical bride through these days.

Each bride's father chooses his own day in this marriage month, consulting the others in order to space the parties over the whole month. During the next weeks they receive their daughter a few times in her new status as a married woman, exchanging food gifts between groom and father. As these feasts draw to an end, the initiation of the boys draws all the attention of the village for the next month. During the complicated ceremonies of this "harvest of men" the newlywed girls join in. The main event, the two-day song festival, gives the girls a rare opportunity to compare their singing and other talents to the others. As this ritual is an integral part of the marriage ceremonies, it shall be described in some detail in the next chapter. This part of the marriage proceedings, however, has many aspects of an initiation. All newlywed girls undergo the rites together; boys coming of age in that year have parallel rites in the same week. This joint initiation of boys and girls is closed at the second day of songs by a rite emphasizing respective clan membership. The boys will become full-fledged adult clan members, and for the girls their village and clan membership will remain the one and only fixed point of reference in their lives of successive marriages, taking them from husband to husband and from village to village.

The new men and new women are still somewhat marginal during the next cultivating season which should start immediately after the end of the rainy season in the big five-day village festival. In these five days the initiated boys parade through the village in full regalia, adorned with feathers, bronze rings, bracelets and pendants. They lead the main dance on the village high ground. Just before the festival each bride receives her own cooking implements and a supply of sorghum and millet grains from her father. She leads a procession of clanswomen and neighbors to her new husband's home proudly displaying the wealth that her father has lavished upon her; this represents her second opportunity to compete against her age mates. The main focus of this festival is neither the boys nor the newlywed brides and grooms, but the "stolen women," the women "stolen" from a different village by a Mogodé man. The proud men who boast a wife "stolen" from an enemy line up and dance before the whole village, their wives behind them. The "harvest of people" includes the newly initiated adults but is not complete without all the women the men from Mogodé have enticed from neighboring villages.

After the "people harvest," the sorghum is reaped in earnest and village life resumes its normal course. The new people are part of the village for the next year and harmony prevails. The whole series of rites should not be considered an expression of unity but rather an instrument to ensure harmony. The ever-present conflicts between men and women, between both village halves, between private and public interests are silent for a moment and the authority of the supernatural world is invoked to instill the Kapsiki with public values of how life should be, but almost never is.

The comparison of the Kapsiki religion with other mountain tribes is more difficult than in the domains of social organization or history. Religions vary more than almost any other cultural domain. Some similarities can be found. The notion of one more-or-less-single God is fairly common as is the manner of sacrifice: an individual and/or family affair, or for special concerns performed by village chiefs. Sacrifice can be found throughout Africa in any tribal religion. It is the central rite of giving to God in order to receive. In various ways and with a multitude of intentions, sacrifices are repeated the world over. The Kapsiki sacrifice is fairly typical, straightforward in its aim, intention and method. Kapsiki religious life seems more individualized than among most other groups. Notably absent from the picture are ancestors. In Kapsiki religion, ancestors do not play any part other than the *melE,* representing deceased parents and used in sacrificial procedure. African traditional religion routinely is characterized as an ancestral religion, but the stereotype does not fit the Kapsiki. It is easy to overestimate the importance of ancestors for African religions in general. The Kapsiki are typical in many other respects. Theirs is a religion for the living not for the dead, geared to the exigencies of social, political and married life, not at the shadowy afterlife the individual is believed to be heading for. So the "harvest of people" — although quite Kapsiki in its details — is in essence a very African trait. People are important, scarce and precious. It should be noted that demographically Kapsiki society is static (Podlewski 1966) due to an exceptionally high infant mortality and a large number of endemic diseases. So insistence on health (in sacrifice) and on people in communal ritual is quite proper.

Kapsiki religion, as any tribal religion, is dwindling with the combined impact of general modernization, Christian missionaries and the pressure of Islam. Although Christian missions have met with limited success (a dozen households are professed Christians in Mogodé), Islam is a more important influence. Modernizing for a Kapsiki often automatically implies Islamization, a process called "Fulanization" in Cameroon. In such cases the Kapsiki like people from all other mountain tribes not only change religion but their entire lifestyle as well. They adopt the customs, clothes, houses and even language of the Fulani, their former enemies—now politically the most important group in North Cameroon. This process can be seen in any town (Schultz 1983) as well as in a village like Mogodé. Around the "chef de canton" a core of "Fulanized" Kapsiki makes up a central ward in the village. Between 1972 and 1984, this ward grew from 20 households to 80. Reasons for Fulanization often are pragmatic in nature: to get a certain job, a political post, to become a representative for the canton chief or to start as a merchant.

5

Women on the Move

We have now established the general historical and social setting of the Kapsiki and we have addressed their manner of thinking and believing. We now turn to the most remarkable aspect of Kapsiki culture: the marriage system. The central issue is the instability of the Kapsiki marriage which stems from the mobility of the women. There are two main types of marriage; the first — a young girl's marriage — will be explored in detail. The first wedding of a girl takes place somewhat before the rainy season and also constitutes the first phase of her initiation. This lasts throughout the rainy season and ends with the large village festival mentioned in Chapter Four.

Rules for choosing a wife are easy in the case of a girl. For the second marriage type — the marriage of a runaway woman — rules are much more intricate. This type of marriage has an entirely different procedure, characterized by a strong antagonism between the consecutive husbands. The difference between the marriage types can be shown in the mean duration of those marriages, which is short by any standard, but varies significantly.

Brideprices play a significant role. Due to the instability of marriage, brideprices not only are paid but often are reclaimed too. For a society where marriage is so short, brideprices are astonishingly high. The network of transactions emanating from marriages is extremely complex. The instability of marriage — and consequently the frequency of contracting new marriages — bears great consequences for both men and women, although the impact on each sex is quite different. The chapter concludes with an exploration of some of the socio-psychological consequences of this marital instability for the relationship between men and women.

In the preceding chapters the subject of marriage inevitably cropped up. No topic is discussed as much in Kapsiki life as marriage. People seemingly never stop thinking, talking or quarrelling about marriages. Men are continually seeking wives, paying brideprice, trying to extract large sums from their sons-in-law, reclaiming brideprices for women who have left them, or trying to stall the repayment of brideprice for wandering daughters. Women deliberate whether they should stay with their present husbands, depart for a new one, how to become pregnant again, etc. Kapsiki society can truly be called a society with a marriage complex. Marriage is extremely brittle; women easily and frequently leave their husbands in search of another, lured by the idea of finding someone new who will supply the riches of life: children, food and sex. Marriage rules, which will be discussed in some detail below, are very explicit: a girl should first marry a boy of her home village. After settling in his compound, she is free to stroll to another man, with the provision that the next husband live in another village. These runaway marriages have been dubbed "second marriages" (Meek 1933) and are contracted with such regularity that many women conduct extensive marriage tours throughout the various Kapsiki villages.

Before examining the marriage types in detail, some factors allowing for the high mobility of the female half of the population should be pointed out. Economically, a woman is quite independent. In the second chapter we saw that a woman has her own cash resources (sometimes more than her husband) and conducts her own business with her own crops. All real estate belongs to men, namely the fields, house, trees, etc. Thus, it would appear that a wife would depend on her husband to furnish her with the means of production. However, no shortage of land exists; resources are open and no man would deny his wife the use of his land. After all, she is producing for him as well as for herself; her gain can become his riches if he plays his cards right. Women have access to as many fields as they want to cultivate, but no woman is ever tied to any specific spot in one village or another. Her own possessions can be moved easily. In a few headloads, all her household goods are easily transported to another compound. She usually converts her crops quickly into cash. As a result of this mobility women know their kith and kin in other villages far better than men do. They live most of their lives among non-kin people; a woman's daughters are spread over the ethnic territory just as she was, while her former husbands are at odds with each other and live in different villages. Her one and only stronghold in life are her male kinsmen: in early life her brothers, later her sons. At the start of her marriage life a woman is guided by her father. He directs her to her first husband and may induce her to leave him for a new one, all the while collecting brideprice as she goes along. After his death her brothers step into his social niche to perform the same functions, but they lack the father's authority and the woman becomes more and more independent. Her relationship with her brothers is usually very good and becomes more equal as the woman is less influenced by them in each successive marriage.

This lack of security regarding a wife's presence in his home compels a man to keep marrying. He needs women for cultivation (women perform a large share of crop cultivation) and for running his household: caring for the children, grinding sorghum, cooking his meals, fetching water and firewood. A man without a woman is a pitiable creature who has to do all these chores himself and will never be able to produce sufficient food to attract a woman.

Men must strive for more than one wife in order to be secure. An intriguing twist is that a wife who has left can always come back and never be refused. Thus it is essential for the whole system to be based on polygamy, more precisely polygyny.

For the women, polygamy might bring about jealousy. However, a co-wife can also provide life-long friendship much more than a husband. Co-wives share everyday activities; they might also learn crafts from each other. For most women, having a co-wife alleviates the tedious tasks of daily life. Thus, a polygamous union can be attractive for a woman — if (and only if) she can get along well with her co-wife.

Vital factors in the marriage complex are children and brideprice. Giving brideprice for the first marriage of a girl is a long, drawn-out process. Brideprice, in fact, extends over the whole reproductive career of the woman. Brideprice is paid to claim the children. After a woman has given birth to one or two children she has — as the Kapsiki expression goes — "repaid" it. Fertility is, therefore, very important.

We shall see that this same insistence on fecundity and its corollaries bring about some of the essential features of the marriage complex. The frequency with which women contract new marriages forces many fathers-in-law to refund the brideprice to a former son-in-law, thus increasing the tensions concerning mobile women. It should be readily apparent that marriage does not cement long-lasting relationships between clans. Kapsiki society is kept divided by the touring women. On the other hand, the sheer number of unions — especially the resulting children — unite the autonomous social units in some way. Of course this situation is not conducive to an intimate relationship between husband and wife. Friction, even antagonism, between the marriage partners is a standard feature of social life.

Marriage Types

The distinction between the first marriage of a girl, her *makwa* marriage, and all her consecutive marriages, called *kwatewume,* pervades marital relations. Both *makwa* and *kwatewume* are nouns indicating the union as well as the woman contracting it. The *makwa* marriage is a girl's first one; in fact *makwa* could be translated as "girl" or "bride." The girl is her father's *makwa,* and the prospective husband *(zamakwa)* and his immediate kin call her so too. During the elaborate ritual of her first married year she stays a *makwa* for the whole village, and in this period the word has also a connotation of initiation. Men are proud to marry a *makwa*, and rightly so, as a *makwa* marriage for a man is quite a feat. Compared to his efforts to obtain a runaway woman, he has truly worked and sweated to marry a *makwa*. He will even call his bride *makwa* long after she has left him for another husband.

The moment a *makwa* leaves her *zamakwa* for her next husband, she becomes a *kwatewume*, literally one for whom the brideprice will be paid. Nearly all women leave their *zamakwa* at some time or another; they may continually seek new husbands. This category of *kwatewume* marriages comprises the greater number of protracted marital unions. However, they are even more brittle than *makwa* unions, as we shall see. Both marriage types represent separate phases in a woman's life, and thus contrast sharply with each other:

Makwa	*Kwatewume*
first marriage	all consecutive marriages
long and elaborate preparation	very short preparation
complex ritual	very little ritualization
brideprice paid in advance	brideprice paid afterwards
protracted in one month each year	protracted at any time
husband is a man from the same village	husband is a man from a different village
few restraints in partner choice	many restrictions in choice
father-in-law vs. son-in-law relationship is important	relationship between the two consecutive husbands is important

Despite differences, both types are valid marriages. However, *kwatewume* unions may be of very short duration, as little as one week or even a few days. The difference between marriage and adultery is often questionable.

The Kapsiki use several expressions to indicate the process of marrying a man and a woman. *Kawume* and *kadzembe cE* apply to both types of marriage. The first verb has a gamut of meanings, the most common being the notion of fertility and ripening. It is used for corn and sorghum ripening in the field, for the consecration of a newly built granary, for the initiation of boys and, last but not least, for marrying a woman. The noun *wume* also means brideprice. *Kadzembe cE* literally means to enter the hut. It indicates a small but vital part in the *makwa* proceedings, but can be used for the entire marriage ritual in both marital types. These verbs point the way to the native definition of a marriage: a woman is considered married to the man in whose hut she resides signifying past or future payment of a brideprice and, if possible, offspring. Whenever a woman runs away to a new spouse, she is considered his wife the moment she enters the entrance in the wall surrounding his castle-like compound. In the wet season, cultivating his fields has the same significance. No divorce procedure exists; a new marriage implies the rupture of the former marital union. A woman who is simply visiting a friend or neighbor behaves very differently; she normally would not enter the compound. A new *kwatewume* marriage has its own procedure and ritual setting clearly different from any other occasion, although the procedure and ritual are not nearly as complex and elaborate as the *makwa* proceedings.

Brideprice is equally vital to residence in defining a marriage. When a daughter or sister resides with her husband, the father or brother can claim the brideprice. In the case of *makwa* this process has been going on for years, whereas for a *kwatewume*, the brideprice is exacted after the birth of children. In any case, the children belong to the man who was married to the woman at the moment of conception, provided he has paid or will pay the brideprice for them. So *pater* and *genitor* usually will be the same person. In principle this holds also for very short marriages, but difficulties may arise. The woman in question will give birth in the compound of her new husband, who is only too happy to have the child. The former husband must therefore lay claim to the child, in former times by religio-magical means, now by resorting to formal courts. His chances are small; the woman will normally corroborate her present husband's counterclaim; her testimony usually wins the judgment. Yet, the value of children is so high that men are willing to take the costly chance. Any children left behind by their mothers are cared for by other wives of the father or by the father's mother.

Although even marriages of one day must be considered valid social unions, adultery can and does occur whenever a woman has sexual intercourse with another man in her husband's compound. This is an extremely serious infringement upon the husband's sexual rights as well as on his essential privacy and calls for a fight between the two men and their kinsmen.

The two types of marriage entail slightly different rights and duties on the partners. The *makwa* bridegroom (the *zamakwa*) has stronger rights and claims on his bride than a consecutive husband, and a *makwa* has more and lasting duties towards her first husband. The differences show when the marital ties are severed. The *zamakwa,* having paid the *wume*, is entitled to at least one of his bride's children. If she has left him and has had children by her new husband, the *zamakwa* can reclaim his money and goats (brideprice) from the former father-in-law who in turn taxes the second son-in-law; the latter will either give one of his children to the *zamakwa* or compensate him for the loss by payment of some kind. When a *makwa* leaves for her next marital stop, her *zamakwa* can seek her out in a strange and hostile village without risking the severe beating a *kwatewume* husband

KwafashE, a *Kwatewume* wife.

will receive if caught doing the same thing (see our opening case). However, the immunity of the *zamakwa* is exhausted after the first attempt if the woman returns again to her new husband. If the *zamakwa* tries to regain his wife a second time, he may be beaten if caught. The *makwa*, for her part, has lasting duties towards her first husband. She must perform several rituals for a deceased *zamakwa,* even if she has left him. She has to stay in his compound for six months, from the date of his death to the final ritual ending the mourning period.

Two variations on both marriage types should be mentioned, the *derheli-*marriage and the *male kezeme rhE.* The first one is the marriage with a young girl before the *makwa* rites are to be contracted. It is tantamount to stealing another man's *makwa* from under his nose. A co-villager lures the girl into his compound, gives the word to her father that he wants to perform the *makwa* instead of her appointed *zamakwa.* If the girl and her parents agree, he quickly pays the brideprice in order to balance the claim of the other man and goes through the marriage rites with her:

> On a bright morning *Ketle,* a young neighbor of ours, announces sadly that he has lost his *makwa.* A man from another ward has stolen her and he is afraid she will stay with him. Bypassers try to cheer him up saying her parents will not agree, but to no avail. Most men easily imagine his chagrin: all that beer, the labor and all those presents just for nothing. It really hurts. Though a week later his prospects of regaining his bride seem a little bit better, *Ketle* is eventually fully justified in his pessimism. His *makwa* never returned to him. Two years later he married another *makwa,* one who did stay some years with him.

When his *makwa* is stolen, a *zamakwa* can only sit tight and wait, hoping his father-in-law will return his bride to him. This does usually happen and most thefts of *makwa* end quickly in the return of the girl to her father, after which she marries her rightful bridegroom. Despite the small chances of success some men try to marry all their *makwa* by means of *derheli.* If it succeeds it is much less work, although the man has gained not only a wife, but also an enemy in the village.

The second variation, *male kezeme rhE,* is widow inheritance. The term means "the woman one eats with the compound." After the death of her husband, a widow can marry one of his younger clan brothers. If she has given her deceased husband any children; i.e., if the *wume* is repaid in kind, she may choose whomever she wants, just like a *kwatewume* marriage, and a new brideprice eventually will be paid. If no children have been born, she is entitled to marry one of his close patrilineal kin and no brideprice is required, an arrangement which is, in fact, a levirate. Most inherited wives are *kwatewume;* if a *zamakwa* dies, the widow will be pressed into a levirate by the brothers, as a *makwa* bond is too valuable to give away.

How to Marry a *Makwa*

Kweji Da nearly stumbles as his right foot hits a hidden rock at the end of the steep, winding trail. With his utmost effort he keeps the huge pot with beer in an uneasy balance on his head. Warning his half brother, *Sunu*, to be careful he halts in front of the compound of *Ndema*, his future father-in-law, who happens also to be ward chief. It is pitch-dark, and the rain just made the path slippery. But the two jars of undiluted, unfiltered beer represent the "beer to greet father-in-law," which should be presented in the small hours of the night, without anyone else knowing. *Kweji* hands his father-in-law the chunk of soda belonging to this gift. *Ndema*, who has been aware of *Kweji's* coming, accepts it, greets both younsters formally and adds: "Why did you come so late at night?" *Kweji* having taken off his shoes in front of his father-in-law, answers: "We have not begun ourselves. It has always been done like this lest people talk of the *makwa* wedding we want to perform." *Ndema* thanks them for presenting him this huge amount of beer, and sends the two young men home. The next morning he filters and dilutes the beer, calls in a few close friends, and informs them of the proposed wedding of his daughter *Kwasewa* with *Kweji Da*.

This is the first time the name of the prospective groom is mentioned to outsiders. Until this moment all transactions between the groom and his in-laws have been conducted in great privacy, if not secrecy. The five-year-old *Kwasewa* in fact has been wooed since her birth. *Kweji's* father has been a good friend of *Ndema*, so procuring the latter's daughter for his son has not been difficult. Several other men have tried it too, and *Ndema* has been very careful to keep the other candidates from knowing his decision. The girl's mother had to give her approval too. About a year ago, *Kweji's* father presented *Ndema* with a small gift of *yisa*, aromated yeasted sorrel, the traditional sign for a marriage proposal, and gave a few loin strings to *Kwasewa's* mother. Although for *Ndema* and his wife the decision has been made, presents from other candidates have not been discouraged.

After this greeting beer, *Ndema* will start to ask for gifts, for parts of the brideprice. No total sum will even be mentioned; if *Kwasewa* will stay with *Kweji* and bear healthy children, *Kweji* will always remain in debt to *Ndema*. Although in the ceremonial exchanges leading up to marriage the bride's father often returns a part of the gifts, on the whole a considerable amount of wealth is transferred to him. *Kweji* will also perform services for *Ndema*, helping him to build and maintain the compound, assisting in any communal labor *Ndema* may organize. The same holds for the girl's mother. The proposed marriage still is officially not public knowledge. The *makwa* preparations have to pass one crucial ceremony in order to become fully known and accepted:

Early in the morning the lineage of *Fama's* in-laws gather in his fore-court. *Rhampa,* a young boy from another clan, wants to marry *Fama's* daughter *Kwadaskwa.* Her *kwesegwe,* mother's brothers, will be consulted today. Of the eight jars of red beer *Rhampa* has brought along, *Fama* will use four to drink at this occasion. The other four are given to the *kwesegwe.* The other traditional gifts of four pieces of soda, four knolls of tobacco, a hen and a rooster are distributed the same way (see Figure 5). The groom-in-spé watches the proceedings from the lowest side of the court, silent and without moving. When *Fama's* in-laws after a lot of discussion have distributed the goods among them, he addresses the bride's real mother's brother who is seated in the place of honor, "This is *Rhampa,* the boy who seeks your daughter (sister's daughter) *Kwadaskwa.* He is a good boy, works his fields hard, and makes no problems. May we go ahead with the *makwa* proceedings? If so, let us drink. Well, in fact, let us drink, as nobody may refuse beer offered. "*Fama's* older agnate *Sunu* corrects him, "Let us hear the *kwesegwe* first; that is what they came for. We can drink afterwards if they give their approval." The girl's mother's brother then reminds *Fama,* "I heard *Rhampa* presented you a sheep for the *kwesegwe.* That should be ours; where is it?" After *Fama's* assurance that the sheep will be given, the *kwesegwe* give their approval, and drinking is under way.

Figure 5: Gift Pattern in Bride Presentation

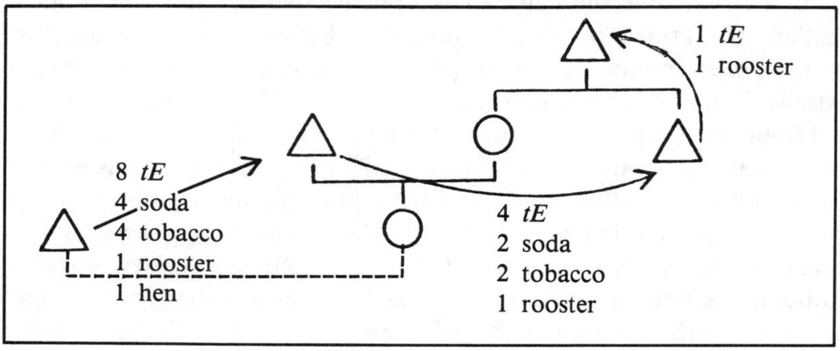

This *tE kwesegwe* went quite smoothly. Sometimes problems may arise, e.g. when a girl's father owes some of the brideprice of the girl's mother. They will scold the father stating, "You eat from our sister, and now you want to eat from our daughter too!" Still more serious problems may arise if the groom or one of his close patrilineal kinsmen, for example, have stolen a wife of one of the mother's brothers, making him an enemy. In that case, the proposed marriage is in danger. However, people are usually very careful whom they seek. From this moment on the intended marriage is public knowledge. The whole village will refer to both partners as *makwa* and *zamakwa* and all other candidates should theoretically despair of obtaining that girl. In reality they do not always, as the *derheli* marriage has shown or because, even more commonly, men from other villages try to persuade the girl to leave her husband-to-be as soon as possible after the wedding. In any case the wedding will proceed. Until the wedding date the groom gives four jars of red beer to his father-in-law each year, who drinks this *tE makwa* with some lineage brothers.

Two years before the eventual wedding the bride comes to stay for six days with her husband-to-be. Accompanied by a little girl from her ward she comes without gifts to his compound and performs all sorts of housekeeping tasks such as fetching water, grinding sorghum or sweeping the floor, but she does not cook. She either sleeps with the groom's mother or with the groom himself, as sexual intercourse is not proscribed. On the last day the *zamakwa* butchers a goat with the assistance of his sister's son. He escorts the two girls back to his *mekwe,* thus ending the *berhe derheli* (to bring away the young girl):

> *Kweji Mte* brings his dear little fiance *Kuve Derha* back to her parents. Both he and his sister's son put their gifts of mush, flour and white beer in the entrance hut and wait till the man of the house addresses them. *Kuve's* father, who has been drinking with a friend, turns towards them and says, "It is well you have brought our daughter back. Of course we agreed in her going to you, as we bear no grudge against you. We have not said anything to you, have we? But there are some problems here; my wife is ill and my brother's wife just miscarried, so there is plenty of work around here. Yet we told the girl to join you. You see, we do not know her attitude *(mehele)* towards you, and as long as we are not sure about her, we cannot really ask you to pay the *wume.* But be sure that the moment we know her mind, we shall ask!" The girl's brother joins in, "You still owe me a goat. It is normal that the *madza* (wife's brother) gets something too; I am the younger brother of your *makwa* and I want a goat." *Kweji Mte,* like a good *zamakwa,* holds his tongue but his companion assures him, "A good father-in-law asks for the brideprice; if not, he will not let his daughter stay in your house."

This happens about two years before the wedding date. In this last period a tug of war takes place between the groom and his father-in-law. The latter tries to stall the marriage as long as possible while the former wants to marry as quickly as possible. After the wedding the claims of the girl's father on additional goats, sheep or clothes making up the brideprice are less strong—in fact he will have to wait for the first child to be born. However, both parties operate within small margins. Normally a girl marries between her fourteenth and sixteenth year, if possible shortly after menarche. A father who has a menstruating daughter in his compound for a longer period will be ridiculed for avarice. Besides, all *makwa* weddings are performed once a year in the same month, just before the new rains. So the real option is whether the girl will marry this season or has to wait still another year.

A series of fixed signals through a formalized gift exchange provides the means of negotiation for both parties. At the start of the last wet season before his desired wedding date, the *zamakwa* starts sowing a field from a full sack of sorghum and hands the rest of the sack over to his *mekwe*. His father-in-law, wanting to stall the wedding, brews red beer from this grain and invites his prospective son-in-law to join him in drinking. If no beer has been brewed, he has agreed with the date. The second signal occurs at the start of the dry season. Then the groom takes five bushels of straw and a big calabash full of flour to the father of his paramour. Acceptance of this gift implies acceptance of the date, and just like the first signal, if the girl's father does not agree, he brews and invites the groom to drink.

If the two above-mentioned signals have been accepted by November, the *zamakwa* carries six jars of red beer to the compound of his fiance. Her father gracefully accepts the gifts, hands half over to the girl's mother and invites her kinsmen and women. One other close relative, often a sister, is of paramount importance in the proceedings. She is called *kweperhwuli*, meaning "She who ties the *cache sexe*," and will escort the girl towards her new home. This day the groom hands her some money to buy several calabashes for the coming rituals. If the bride's father changes his mind and, despite former approval of the date, wants to postpone his daughter's departure, he returns an empty beer jar. Normally, empty jars are never given back.

Throughout the many years of *makwa* preparation, the groom has given a fair number of ceremonial gifts to his father-in-law, in addition to money, goats and other substantial *wume* payments. Three phases in all these procedures may be discerned. The first one starts when the girl is about four years old — after the critical stage of high mortality. It extends through her eighth year; *Kewufuru* (hidden, private) is the Kapsiki term characterizing this period. Well hidden it surely is, but it is not absolutely secret. People talk about it and may be present at the functions. Beer is brought at night, in pitch darkness. It is white beer which can be brewed by women without anybody noticing it, and no lineage members or other kinsmen are consulted or invited to drink. Help in cultivation is given when the prospective groom can be lost in a host of other workers. In these years the girl's father has maximum leeway to demand gifts from as many candidates as he can, hoping with good reason that not all of them will claim their money or gifts.

The second phase starts with the *tE kwesegwe*. For the first time the news of the marriage is spread to a wider audience. People are invited in and the transaction becomes a more social affair. In this latter period beer gifts comprise *tE*, red beer, which is the ritual beer brewed by men. Brewing red beer is a laborious process hardly to be concealed from neighbors and when a man brews his *te* there is something important at hand.

Now that all people concerned agree on the proposed marriage in principle, the wedding season and date still have to be fixed, and the negotiations on this problem constitute the last phase. Starting as a private exchange between just the two men it extends into a full-fledged social affair in which the reluctant approval of the girl's father is extracted through the pressure of his wife's kinsmen. At last people look forward to the end of the year for the wedding to take place.

The Wedding

All *makwa* weddings are held in the same month, each on a separate day of this *tere makwa* (bride moon), usually in April. Starting at the new moon, the village is full of feasting people. Discussions grow heated over a good pot of beer. People come from one and go towards another *verhe makwa*, as these weddings are called. The date of the wedding ceremony is set by the groom who consults his smith-diviner to pick an auspicious day. He then summons his friends and lineage brothers to help him in preparations.

Two things are called for in feasts: beer and meat. Huge quantities of red beer are brewed by the groom and his helpmates; a week before the wedding the bridegroom has his sister's sons butcher a cow or bull on his behalf. During the last fortnight before the wedding he finishes the hut where his bride will live; usually it is the hut of a former wife who left his compound some time ago. Two days before the festival little girls from his ward help him in plastering the entrance with termite earth, to make it smooth and red. When all is finished, the *zamakwa* has some women bring four jars of red beer to his father-in-law, as a signal that all preparations are made, and that his daughter will be transferred from the compound of her birth to the new one of her husband.

The husband being ready, this next day is set apart for the preparation of the bride. In the morning some women of clan brothers assemble in the entrance hut of the girl's father to arrange the *livu*, the chain skirt that is a vital part of the bridal outfit, and to make the *rhwuli*, the *cache sexe* made of bean fibers. The women spend an agreeable afternoon at this light task, drinking at least two jars of red beer from the four the *zamakwa* has brought, and they always bother the girl's father for more. When finished, the oldest women present and the mother's sister dedicate the skirt by spitting beer over it and saying something like: "You should pay the brideprice quickly, so have children fast." The bride herself is not present. She has her head shaved at the blacksmith's and stays in her hut the rest of the day. At dusk she heads for the nearby well together with a small girl from her ward. The little girl ties the iron skirt around her waist and washes it that way. After washing herself the *makwa* puts on her *livu* and is ready for the night's proceedings.

A busy night follows in which the bride is ritually transferred from her father's compound to that of her husband. At sunset friends and clan members of the groom gather in his house, drinking some beer; an occasional blacksmith plays his guitar and hums a praise song to the groom, who is "so generous, so open-handed, and proves himself so rich." Women of the groom's clan exhort him to go and get his wife, singing, "Mother, father give us the child for the rain is coming." When it is completely dark, one of these women is given a calabash with flour, meat, a tiny sacrificial jar and a chicken by the groom's aide, his sister's son. She leads the whole party towards the girl's compound, *kahka makwa*, to call the bride. Children carry five or seven small jars filled with beer, which they put into the forecourt of the girl's home. A few daring boys drink the beer but are soon chased by the children from the bride's ward. If they are caught inside the forecourt, the groom has to set them free with a big additional jar of beer. The accompanying children sing outside the house, "Give us the woman; those who call the *makwa* have arrived and sit under the firewood. Chief of the sun, give your daughter before nightfall."

The Kapsiki classify this part of the proceedings as amusement, a part to be deleted if divination calls for a solemn procedure. In the meantime, however, the women leading the troupe has handed her gifts to *kweperhwuli*, the mother's sister of *makwa*, who will lead the bride to her new house. Inside the *rhE*; i.e., the wall, the girl's father performs a sacrifice to ensure good luck in the transferral, to guarantee a smooth procedure and to enhance the fertility of the bride. As always, details depend on divination:

> *TerimcE* the father of bride *Kuve*, learned from the diviner that the proceedings would have to be quiet: no quarrels, no amusement. *Kuve* should sacrifice a ball of white flour. *TerimcE* has to put some meat from a female and a male animal mixed with flour in his brewery. This is all done while at the background the shrill voices are heard: "Mother of the Sun, give us the bride as it is already dark outside." Later the two groups of women, the groom's against the girl's father's clan, join the singing to abuse each other in derisive songs.

For the last time *TerimcE* tries to stall his daughter's departure, referring to instructions from the diviner, trying to gain some extra gifts from the groom's party. Just before midnight all discussions about the coming of the *makwa* between *TerimcE* and the groom's aide cease as *Kuve* steps out of the exit into the forecourt. Clad in her *livu* cache sexe and a straw rain cape she kneels in the entrance, face inwards to receive her father's blessings.

Suddenly all people grow very quiet; *TerimcE* takes a mouthful of beer, spits it over her saying:

> You are stubborn; when I talk to you, you turn your back. It is better for you not to cross the river in this mood, to go to your husband. I never laid my hands upon you, but a husband is not a father. You are in your father's house no longer, and you are not the only one in the new compound. Many people live over there. I want things to go right. I want you to stay in that compound till you die and I do want you pregnant immediately. Only then I can explain everything to you, and, if there may be a reason, give you to another man. I want you to work hard, to give your sex to your husband, in order to be pregnant. That is what I want.

He again spits a mouthful of beer over her. *Kuve* does not say a word, but has her *kweperhwuli* guide her to the *zamakwa's* home. A little boy from her father's ward walks near her.

Near the compound of the groom, a friend or clan brother of the bride's father living close by will watch over her well-being, will serve as her *yitiyaberhe* (accompanying father). He is a kind of "ward father" to whom she can flee if marriage problems become too many, if her husband does not fulfill his matrimonial duties or beats her too hard. This second father has also received beer from the groom and gives the bride a similar blessing. In the above-mentioned case he said, "Put forth two pairs of twins, and then I shall give you to another man."

Silently and alone the girl enters the groom's hut to perform a sacrifice inside her new home similar to the sacrifice she has attended in her father's home. When this is done she joins her mother's sister who is waiting outside, surrounded by many interested and curious people. As she has only entered the compound in order to assist at the sacrifice, she has not "officially" entered the house yet. In the pitch-dark of the night an amusing interlude follows in which the assistant of the groom tries to motivate the girl's companion, her mother's sister, to enter the house with *makwa*. He may not force her nor make her angry, but has to use sweet words and presents. The giving party clearly shows itself socially superior to the recipient, the groom's companion. Most *kweperhwuli* really savor the situation, make the most of it by pocketing money and giving a running commentary on the defects of the groom, his kin and any bystanders. At last, of course, both women plus the little boy have to enter the compound to halt again before entering the bride's hut. After some last gifts they finally install themselves in the newly prepared hut, where *makwa* takes off her rain mat and busies herself the rest of the night grinding sorghum and sweeping the floor. The bridegroom has a little girl from his compound or ward join his bride as a companion, but does not show up himself. He should not yet see his bride; if this *makwa* is his first bride, he stays the night at a friend's home to return late the next day.

Entering the hut has been the critical point in the marriage; by entering her new abode the girl is considered married to her husband. In fact, the term used to indicate the first marriage of a girl other than *makwa* is *kadzembe cE* (to enter the hut). As with any Kapsiki ritual a private phase precedes a public festival in which the community participates. In the ceremony of calling for the bride, the ascendancy of the bride's family is clearly expressed: the groom's party comes to solicit the gift of the bride; the girl's father stalls as long as he can and so does the mother's sister before entering the home. Throughout the wedding the girl's family should never be angered or irritated as during the wedding the bride's kin wields power over her fertility. If the father of the bride should be discontent, his daughter will either be infertile or will leave her husband very soon.

The next day a big feast is held. The whole ward and both lineages of the groom and the girl are well-represented. Since other wedding feasts are probably held on the same day, some people may have to choose which feast they will attend. All guests bring some mush and beer as a gift, "to greet *makwa,*" and the lineage members of the groom show up with huge quantities of sorghum. From the early morning the compound is crowded with people drinking, walking, gossiping and eating. Among all guests three groups of people are of prime importance: the group of the groom's mother's brothers, the bride's family and the old men of the ward. They are served with great care by the groom's sister's sons who organize the whole procedure. The women of both clans engage in a kind of corporate song contest, in which the groom's party insults the *makwa* in song and exhorts her to bring forth many children: "You beat the people. You think you are important in the house now, but wait and see! You think you are going to sleep on an iron bed, but you will sleep on the floor. Better have some twins!" The other party counters with: "The groom is poor and and has the head of a vulture. He could not even repair the hut well. *Makwa,* you are a girl from the sun; when he beats you, allow him to do so only with a millet stalk. Flee to your hut, or, even better, come with us back to your home."

The morning is filled with drinking, singing and other amusement while the women of the groom's ward cook the meal. No wedding is without meat. Mush has been cooked in advance. In the afternoon all guests are served and eat their fill, save for two representatives among the groom's mother's brothers. While the others from that party eat abundantly, the groom presents them with four jars of the best beer, makes a little speech saying he hopes they are content with the marriage and with the wedding feast. His kinsmen answer in the affirmative, and give some money and iron bars to assist in the expenses, the whole group making up for some 3000 CFA ($10) and a dozen bars of iron (a traditional object of exchange). The first beer is poured from the sacrificial jar into a calabash and the ward chief pours some beer on the ground as a libation, saying (e.g.), "She has to give a girl and another girl. We pour for those who are dead. If anybody wants to do harm, let him be lamed. May the man marry scores of brides after this one.''

The libation being done, the groom passes a calabash of beer around the circle and has all his mother's brothers spit into it. Then the two that have refrained from eating thus far take the calabash into the *makwa's* hut where the bride kneels in the door opening clad in her full attire: chain skirts and cape. One after the other both men take a mouth full of beer, spit the beer over the kneeling girl saying: "Be healthy, have many children and pay the brideprice. One after the other." Then *makwa* has to empty the calabash.

During the preparation of the meal a "test" on the virginity of the *makwa* has been performed. A chicken, slaughtered by the old men of the ward, is cleaned and then sewn tight with bean fibers and thus left to dry. If its belly splits open during the day, the *makwa* has not been faithful to her husband-to-be. Although no sanctions follow such a discovery, it dims the festive spirit of the occasion. When all is well and the seam stays tight, the chicken is shown to the bride's mother's sister and the father. With this assurance they return home; the woman takes several gifts to her house from the groom and the girl's father, after eating in his own compound, awaits the farewell gifts to which he is entitled.

When the sun begins to set, the "bridal-maiden" chicken is cooked and eaten by the old men of the ward, while the mother's brothers receive a chicken from the groom's assistant and leave the compound singing lewd songs. When at last the old men leave, the party is over. Only a few friends stay with the groom. Two of them have just carried the gifts of mush, meat and sauce to the bride's father. In the falling dusk the friend at whose *rhE* the groom spent the night has his wives carry two jars of white beer to the festive compound, for the *kwageze rhena* (to speak words) — the start of communication between husband and wife, verbal and other:

> While his friends drink the beer in the forecourt, the groom *Zera* joins his *makwa* who has seated herself in the back of the groom's personal hut. *Kuve* throws her bracelet to her husband, who remains in the door, with the words "Here are your things." He throws it back, and after repeating this they start talking with each other, leading to sexual intercourse.

At this time the marriage union is forged and socially approved, but this elaborate ceremony just marks the start of a period in which the bride still is marginal in her new household. In fact this "period of marginality" will last until the huge village festival at the close of the wet season, about five months later. So for this whole agricultural season the bride stays *makwa*, enjoying special attention from her new "lord and master," but subject to a fair number of behavioral proscriptions. Thus, she may not whistle nor relieve herself in the fields lest she damage the crops. Her behavior, as well as the doings of the newly initiated boys, directly affects the growing crops. This relation between marriage (and initiation) and agricultural fertility will show up again in the village festival at the end of the season.

The marginal status of the girl can be seen too in the way she shuttles between her father and her husband in the first week of her marriage. After the wedding the *makwa* stays four days within the nuptial compound. In the meantime her husband has gifts presented to her mother's brother, to her father, and to the little boy and girl who have assisted her during the wedding. After four days the *makwa* starts carrying gifts of mush, meat and peanut sauce for her father. She stays two nights and two days at her father's and when she leaves him he gives her about the same amount of food to present to her husband. In all her doings the *makwa* is accompanied by a little boy of her husband's kin. She goes back to her husband's compound and stays four days before leaving again for her father with gifts from her husband. This last time she leaves after two days, with peanuts and millet to grind at home. The next day, back at her new home again, she leaves the compound for the first time to go into the bush to fetch some leaves for that night's mush sauce. She gradually becomes more mobile; from now on she may leave the compound to fetch water, collect firewood or go on any other errand. Now that her relationship with her father has been gradually settled in this period of social weaning, she has to build up relationships with the groom's kin. Her husband will direct her in this, telling her to whom she must present gifts of *rhwempe* (a mixture of ground peanuts and couch). Usually his father, mother, mother's brother and a lineage elder are among the first. The girl presents her gifts tacitly, gets some money in return, and only starts communicating with them after this little gift exchange. A farewell gift to the little boy who has followed her throughout ends the period of gradual separation from her family. In due course she regains some of the mobility she had before marriage, but now as a married woman who can walk around as she likes to visit markets, to gossip with friends or to become acquainted with a prospective new husband.

Figure 6: Wedding Scheme

	Groom	**Bride**
2 days before wedding	builds hut brews beer butchers cow finishes hut brings beer to father-in- law consults diviner	father consults diviner has her head shaven skirt and *cache sexe* made and washed

	Groom	Bride
1 day before wedding evening	has his bride called	receives blessing from father enters husband's compound
wedding day	receives guests	receives guests has virginity "tested"
4 days after wedding	starts "speaking words"	starts "speaking words" brings gifts to father-in-law
4-6 days after wedding		stays with her father
6-10 days after wedding		stays with her groom
10-12 days after wedding		stays with her father
13 days after wedding		goes into the bush
14 days after wedding		brings gifts to husband's kin

Initiation

Thus far the wedding has been in fact an individual affair, centering around two people, groom and bride. Although kinsmen of both play an important role in the proceedings, kin groups hardly function as a whole in the ceremonies. This is different in the second phase of the wedding, which we call "initiation." All girls married in the *makwa* month go through the initiation phase as a group, together with the boys that pass through initiation that year (see Chapter Four).

At the start of the following month, which should be the first month of the rainy season, the boys coming of age this year begin their initiation rituals under tutelage of their elder brothers. As a central feature of this initiation each boy is ceremonially locked in his newly provided personal hut for eight days. After this eight-day period the main collective rituals are held in which all *makwa* also take part and which for them constitute the second part of the wedding. In the early morning of the last day of the boys' confinement, all newly married girls gather at the compound of the chief smith, clad in their chain skirt and leather belt. A little girl accompanies each of them, carrying food for the *makwa*. These little girls are clad in a string of iron beads, of which they give four beads to the smith's wife as payment for the operation her husband is about to perform. The blacksmith shaves each *makwa's* head so as to leave a kind of helmet-like patch and makes four incisions at the base of her belly. These incisions are intended to become cicatrixes to be shown proudly to her husband and kinsmen. The girls are helped according to their groom's clan membership: first the girls married to men from the first phratry, those of the other phratry afterwards. When all are finished, they walk as a group towards one of the central mountains in Mogodé, *Rhwemetla,* a volcanic outcropping sacred for several reasons. All girls halt some hundred meters before the mountain, get their meal from their helpers and eat their mush kneeling on several flat stones (the normal way of eating is in a squatting position). Their husbands gave them this meal, expressing satisfaction with their bride (thus far) through a white-colored mush (from rice), or dissatisfaction through red mush (sorghum). However, white mush is nearly always given, as any public announcement of discontent would be a strong motive for a girl to leave her husband. No sane husband would want that after going through that much trouble and expense.

After finishing their meal, the girls approach the mountain cautiously and kneel in single file about thirty meters before their destination, a small cavern at the base of the granite mass. They take off their skirts and the girl who has had the earliest wedding leads the way in, creeping towards the entrance of the cavern. This is the most solemn moment of the day; the girls are anxious not to make a mistake. The leading girl sets in with the song belonging to this occasion, *laliyama,* the other girls repeating in unison after her:

> *Laliyama* (greetings)
> It is my grandfather's habit
> It is the custom of *Zera* (her father)
> We did not start it
> These things are from the people of old
> these things are from the people of ages past
> *Laliyama*
> I did not commence this
> These are the things of the mountain people
> these are the things of the *kagwenji* (clan)
> these are the things of the people on *Rhungwedu* (ancestral mountain)
> these are the things of people with many cattle
> these are the things of my mother *Kuve*
> these are the things of the ancestors of those who sacrifice
> these are the things of the people of *ZagwayE* (ancestor)
> these are the things of the people of *Lakwa* (old name of the village well)
> be greeted rich people
> be greeted (*lale*) well
> be greeted things of the village founders
> be greeted performers of the village sacrifice
> I did not start it.

When near the cavern, all girls suddenly run towards it to secure a good place at the entrance. Now one of the socially culminating events is to take place: a kind of song contest between the girls. This whole day and the following one will be spent by the girls singing at the cave entrance. A huge crowd of village people surrounds them to hear how the *makwa* improvise their songs. Skillful improvisation with derisive remarks about outsiders

This year's newlywed girls assemble their food before entering the culminating ritual of their initiation.

and flattering praise on kinsmen and affines are highly valued. The spectators and listeners really savor the girls' efforts to outdo each other in extolling the heroic deeds of their ancestors, to boast about the riches of their husbands and to poke fun at girls who are less adept in this game. Flattered husbands give their brides some money by pressing coins on their shining foreheads, while a poor singer's mother complains, "Who is going to mourn over me when I am dead"; if they feel they can die in peace they give money too. A few examples of some lines:

> Greetings, *Masi,* greetings *Masi kwarumba* (her mother)
> *Masi,* daughter of the chief
> Even the boys of Douala talk about me
> When the girls from the bush arrive, the feast is done
> If one could die from words, I would be long dead
> Be silent, you slaves, I am speaking
> Wait a moment, I am going to win the festival
> Among us *makwiyE* (clan) there are few who make mistakes
> If no *Teruza* (sublineage) is present, there is no village
> These are the people of my mother
> Be welcome, *Kweji Nzama.* Why do you look at me?
> I have called the whole day, why do you show up so late
> Why did you not buy me some clothes
> I am going home, just wait and see.

All these lines are repeated by the whole chorus of girls interspersed with *yayE,* an exclamation without specific significance. Through *yayE* songs take up most of the day, some songs of a more ritual kind are sung during the proceedings in which the girls acknowledge the ancestors, the founders of the village of old, the authorities of the village and the spirit of the mountains.

One hour before sunset the girls stop singing, leave their niche at the cavern and descend to the nearby well to wash themselves, wearing their iron skirts. This washing down is called *kapE dEgwu,* to wash away the youth. Girls that sang well deride the less adept ones, and their little helpers do the same. They then head for their husbands.

The next day marks the culmination of the festivities. The boy initiates perform a complicated ritual (van Beek 1978:327-330) the latter part of which coincides with that of the girls. The girls' program is almost the same as the day before; they have their cicatrices remade at the blacksmith's and eat their mush before singing the whole day long at the cavern entrance. When they start singing, the boys commence their rituals for this day, a busy day for them. A huge crowd assembles at the cave and the colorful crowd of singing girls and their married onlookers and admirers make for a festive ambiance. After five o'clock the *gewela,* boy initiandi, ask the girls to join them at their abode, an inclining rock some hundred meters towards the east. After two customary refusals, the boys throw stones at a wasp nest

The start of the singing contest for this year's newlywed girls.

not too far from the girls cave, and the *makwa* rush from their seats towards the boys' rock. A well with a small pool marks half way, where the girls dip their right foot into the water, and put a calabash they have been carrying on their head. At the rock, called *Mentsehe,* they are fed some mush by a boy of their clan. A few old men from the village now supervise the proceedings as the culminating rituals of the boys' and girls' initiation are about to be performed. *Gewela* and *makwa* gather at the small boulder lying thirty meters from *Mentsehe* and when the path between the two landmarks is cleared, the boys and girls start running from the boulder to *Mentsehe* and back; each time two boys and two girls or a boy and a girl (the two of them always from the same clan) run two or four times the distance, touching the rocks with their right foot. If one of them stumbles, an official makes two cuts on his or her forearm to avoid the misfortune that would inevitably follow the clumsiness. When their course is run, the boys leave for a tour over the sites of ancestral exploits; the girls and their helpers eat the mush and return home.

If the timing is correct, the first rains fall during the initiation ceremonies. After initiation the work on the fields starts. At this season *makwa* as well as *gewela* should cultivate as much as possible; they should be fruitful and productive, and should behave circumspectedly and act cautiously, avoiding loud laughter or disputes. Throughout the rainy season the girls are addressed as *makwa*, and they perform all domestic and nuptial duties (with one proviso that will be discussed below).

After the rains and just before the harvest of the sorghum, the great village festival is held, concluding the initiation period for both boys and girls. It is a five-day festival in which the whole village and many visitors from neighboring villages participate. Since the village feasts are held in a fixed sequence from one village to the other, "strangers" can be present without missing their own concluding cyclic rituals.

Although the main focus of this ritual is "the harvest of people" (van Beek 1978:334); i.e., married girls and the boys who have grown up that year, the husbands feature prominently in the festivities. The main attention is theirs and the glory is theirs. The men that have managed to marry a runaway woman *(kwatewume)* this year dress up in fabulous attire with lots of sashes, scarfs and bells and lead the dance as a group. However, the *zamakwa* has more work to do. He starts early and brews large quantities of red beer (more than 300 liters is not unusual). In a small ceremony, friends help him construct the lean-to belonging to the bride's hut. He pays for the help with beer and then presents four jars of beer to his father-in-law. His bride has just arrived at her father's house, clad in the iron skirt and a leather bracelet with one cowry shell.

The *makwa* stays that night at her father's compound — the last night she will normally ever spend there. The next morning a *makwa's* father presents her dowry, a custom called *berhe makwa*, to accompany the bride. Early in the morning, while the first curious visitors assemble in the forecourt, the women of the house take out all the goods the father wants to bestow upon his daughter: big calabashes with sorghum and millet, meat, honey and many other things.

> Dowry of *KwayEngu Kwada*:
> 29 calabashes with sorghum and millet
> 2 baskets with small decorated calabashes
> 2 baskets with meat
>   various enamel bowls
>   pottery bowls
>   a plaited mat for presenting mush
>   a ball of soda
>   two little jars of honey
>   a sack of salt
>   two sticks for stirring the mush

Two-thirds of the sorghum is a gift from the *KwayEngu's* father, the remaining third is given by her mother. Meanwhile the women from the groom's ward have arrived to carry the whole dowry away, but before they can put the bride's wealth on their heads, the *makwa* protests vigorously. The dowry is too small. Although the dowry is quite sumptuous in this case, a bride has to voice some protest. *KwayEngu's* mother takes a big calabash from her hut and challenges her husband to fill it, a challenge he has to meet. With this addition the whole party sets out towards the groom's compound, walking in a long file behind *KwayEngu* herself. Before entering the nuptial compound, a stop may be made at the local guardian of the bride, for some beer and a short rest. But in this case the groom lives close by. When the whole party enters the groom's compound, the bride heads straight for her hut whereas the other women yell and scream, "Go and take your beer dregs from the granary; we want to put first-class sorghum in it." Yet all dowry goods are put in the personal hut of the *makwa* to be at her disposal. Meanwhile some women engage in a friendly game of romps, trying to extinguish the cooking fires in the house in order to rekindle them with their own fire.

The groom, who has been awaiting his bride's party in his compound, proudly views the coming riches, gives the women a friendly farewell with some honey and beer. A little boy from her father's lineage stays in the hut of *makwa*. He has a small but vital role in the coming ceremonies. A few women wait for a goat to be slaughtered by the *zamakwa* and take its head and two legs to the girl's father. Before leaving, one of these women takes the girl's right hand and puts it into a jar of water saying, "Now, you have enough to cook, so cook your husband's meal." For that has been the one exception in the domestic chores: *KwayEngu* has not yet cooked for her husband; all his meals have been prepared by her co-wives.

One small ritual remains for the *makwa*. After the women leave, the bride and her husband join the crowd of villagers that wait for the big annual dance to begin. The last event before the feast is the concluding ritual of the boys, who, in a complicated rite, cross a little brook in the heart of the village. All *makwa* come to view the proceedings and the conclusion of their initiation immediately follows that of the boys'. After the crossing, the *makwa* pretend to start for their father's homes, but the little boys from their father's wards take them by the fibres hanging over their buttocks and force them back to their husbands. On the evening of this concluding festive wedding day the *makwa* prepares meat, mush and peanuts, filters beer and

A newlywed girl—with umbrella—together with some women of her neighborhood are about to carry her dowry to her husband's compound.

honey and cooks sauce. Using her best calabashes and dishes, she takes all the delicacies to her husband's hut. Both her little helpers, boy and girl, sleep in her hut, while the bride, who is now fully and formally wed at last, stays the night in her husband's hut. During this day, and in the days that follow, her husband dances in the big all-village celebration that concludes these rites. Clad in big gowns all *zamakwa* of the year circle the multi-colored mass of other husbands and "stolen" women who form the core of the festival. Somewhat on the outskirts of the prancing masses, the *makwa* roam the dancing crowds, clad in their iron aprons and bean-fiber cache sexes. Their runaway sisters are much more important in the proceedings, but the *makwa* have enjoyed their share of ritual attention.

> Patterns of marriage festivities vary widely in Africa, but also in the Mandara area. The Kapsiki case is peculiar in several respects. The first difference is the first marriage of a girl fixed by an agricultural ritual calendar. Protacting marriages once per year is not common at all. Secondly, the sequence of marriage and initiation is a reversal of the usual procedure. In many parts of Africa girls are initiated, but usually before marriage, not after. The parallel boys' and brides' initiation is peculiar too. In our view it is linked to the tendency of the Kapsiki to establish a fixed date for as many rituals as possible. As a whole, the initiation of boys and brides at the same time makes sense within Kapsiki religion: it is a harvest of new adults (see Chapter Four).

Choosing a Spouse

Informants often point out that a man can marry anyone's daughter as a *makwa*, a statement not literally true but socially very relevant, as the presumed liberty in choosing a *makwa* contrasts sharply with the manifold rules restricting choice of a runaway spouse. For *makwa* marriage, exogamy rules prohibit marriage between lineage members or second cousins. In fact this limited rule does not present much of a restriction on the marriage market, because special ritual regulations exist for unions between close kin. If a *makwa* marries someone who is in some way related to her (although not close enough to violate established rules), her children might suffer some risks from the kinship relation of their parents. However, a simple ritual after the birth of the first child will guard against that.

Other rules are far more important. Any *makwa* should marry within the village, if possible. Although not an absolute rule, this village endogamy is firmly entrenched in social life and presents a striking contrast with the village exogamy of the secondary marriage. Eighty percent of all *makwa* marry with a village member, whereas (in Mogodé) 76% of the second marriages are contracted with a man from another village. People are quite explicit on this rule:

> *Kuve Meha,* a girl of about 15, has received a marriage proposal from a boy from Roumsou. However, she already has a *zamakwa, Teri Mte,* from Mogodé. *Kuve* tells her Roumsou admirer that she will perform the *makwa* with Teri first and run away to Roumsou at the first possible option after the rites. That is exactly the way it happens. Five years later, she will leave Roumsou for a new husband in Sena.

> To balance the scale between the two villages, *Zera Fama* from Mogodé wanted to marry *KwayEngu,* the daughter of the village headman of Roumsou, *Ndewuva.* As his other daughters have already left the village shortly after marriage, *Ndewuva* feels his village people grow sensitive on the issue, as a chief's family should stay in the village. Although he is quite happy with *Zera Fama* as a son-in-law, because *Zera* will have a well-paid government job in the near future and will be able to pay a very handsome brideprice, *Ndewuva* induces his daughter to marry another Roumsou husband first with the intention of leaving him shortly afterwards for *Zera Fama* in Mogodé.

Although not nearly as strong as the village endogamy, a tendency towards phratrie endogamy can be asserted too. Women from the first phratry tend to marry men from that phratry more than from the second one and vice versa. The tendency for restricted endogamy in *makwa* marriages culminates in the possibility of *kantsa riki,* "to pick the footpath," meaning marriage within one clan. When all *makwa* preparations and endeavors with girls from other clans fall through, a disappointed candidate turns in exasperation towards his own clan who cannot refuse a brother's claim. Often the brideprice is kept very low since the main purpose is to marry off that too-long single brother.

One clan in Mogodé is quite renowned for marrying its own daughters, the above-mentioned *makwajE* clan. This very same clan also has a reputation for fierceness. The record of past conflicts (including manslaughter) with other Mogodé clans easily accounts for severed relations and renders negotiations on brideprice almost impossible.

In the above case the girl has proved an important factor in making the match. Although "officially" her father picks her *zamakwa,* the girl has a big say in the matter. Fathers of *makwa* do realize that some marriage stability greatly enhances their chances of profit; so it is better not to force their daughter towards a husband she does not want. Kapsiki women are, after all, too independent to be pushed around.

The rules for a *kwatewume* marriage are just the opposite of those relating the choice of the *makwa.* Although lineage and second cousin exogamy pertain in this marriage type also, other restrictions are far more important. The relationship between the two consecutive husbands is crucial. These two men are each other's *zamale* (husband of the wife), an expression almost synonymous with "enemy." One should therefore avoid marrying the ex-wife of anyone with whom one cannot afford enmity, in fact of anyone linked by strong ties. This principle accounts for the following interdictions:

One should not marry the wife of:

- a mother's brother (*kwesegwe*), real or classificatory, in one's own village or "second father" of the man (see below)
- a (classificatory) father's mother's brother
- a ward member
- a *menu* (someone who is sister's son to the same clan as oneself)
- a clan member, and preferably not a phratry member
- a man from one's *hwelefwe* (matrilateral kin, see Chapter Five)
- a friend
- a clan member of the (classificatory) grandparents
- one's family-in-law
- a ritual ally

This whole gamut of rules usually implies that one should avoid marrying a co-villager's wife. Especially in small villages, women must go to another village; no one in their resident village will be able to marry them. Even in other villages, a runaway woman has to look carefully, as her former husband's in-laws and matrilateral kin may be dispersed widely over the whole ethnic territory. She may not be aware of those ties. It is possible that her new husband, on learning whose wife she has been, will have to send her away if he is not in a position to be *zamale* with that man.

This touchy relationship between the husbands of the same woman does not extend over all of her previous mates; it concerns only each pair of consecutive marriage partners. For the third husband, the first one is no threat or competition. Thus, the woman might return to the same village after additional marriages. However, the enmity among *zamale* remains after the woman has left for a third husband. Although the years quell the hostility, contact between the two men will never be easy. The tensions generated by the *kwatewume* marriages may affect the choice of other brides, both *makwa* and *kwatewume,* as one cannot possibly marry the daughter of someone who is himself a *zamale* or closely related to a *zamale:*

> *Kweji,* a member of the *NgacE* clan in Mogodé, tried to marry *KwayEngu,* who is a clan sister of *Teri, zamale* to *Kweji's* brother *Deli.* As the *zamale* relation extends to the close kinsmen, *Kweji* is considered an enemy of *Teri* and *KwayEngu's* father, so the marriage could not take place.

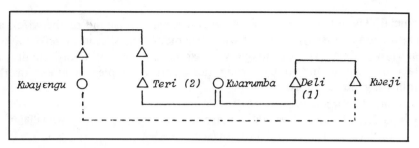

The same holds true in reverse. When one has married a daughter of one village, lots of people are *mekwe* in that village and one should not casually steal a wife from someone over there. So on the whole men tend to marry wives from different villages. In this way, hostilities towards one village will not accumulate too much. A second consequence is the absence of privileged marriage relations between villages; neither between the clans within one village nor between villages do marriage connubia exist. For the Kapsiki marriage is a one-time affair, each union forming and severing its own ties without reference to marriages of past generations—each man for himself, in love and marriage.

Women on the Move

We have concentrated mainly on the male side of the picture. A man's relation with the former husband of his wife is crucial in the way *kwatewume* unions structure social space. Nevertheless the woman takes the initiative for any secondary marriage. When she wants to leave her husband, she simply walks towards another village, often on market day so she can combine business with marriage. After selling her things, she looks for a matrilateral relative, who will house her that night. In the coming marriage he will be her *yitiyaberhe,* literally "father who brings her" or her proxy father, a position comparable to that of the *makwa* second father, but more important. His task is to see that she picks a good husband. Afterwards he has to guard her against any abuse, thus providing her with a stronghold in a strange and often hostile village. If her new husband refuses to give her meat or sorghum or beats her up too much, it is to this kinsman's compound that she will flee to complain. She will call him father, her husband addresses him as *mekwe* (father-in-law) and for her future children he shall be *shi* (grandparent) while his own children are *kwesegwe* (mother's brother) for them. By this institution of proxy fatherhood all women (and their children) are provided with their own kinsmen in each village, replacing the real ones who are living faraway in hostile countryside.

The kinsman of a runaway woman who has announced her intention to marry gives the word to his ward members, friends and kinsmen. Whoever wishes to be a candidate has his women or his friend's women cook mush, meat and beer, and he takes this the next morning as a gift to the proxy father, assisted by some friends and clan brothers. So, during this day, about half-a-dozen candidates assemble in the compound of the woman's kinsman, each with his own clique. The different groups keep well to themselves, eyeing their competitors with suspicion and bitterness, because for the moment they are *zamale* of each other. Each of the parties hands some money to the woman of the house. She plays a pivotal role in the proceedings. She has easy access to the bride-to-be, who also hears all the village gossip through her. She gets to know which of the men is poor, which one is left quickly by all his wives, and which one has so many women that any new one will get lost in the crowd. Often the newly arrived bride knows practically nothing about her new village, so this kind of information will be decisive. The following is an example of the procedure:

> A woman from Garta, *Kwarumba,* arrives in Mogodé at the house of her MoMoBrDaSo *TizhE Kwada.* She left her husband in Garta at the instigation of her father; as she has given her husband four living children, his *wume* is more than repaid and only a new husband will bring some additional gains. Among the Mogodé men *Zera Dumu* wants to pose his candidacy. As he is single, a friend's wife helps him cook the food. Coming in to *TizhE's* spacious and well-built compound, *Zera* and his four friends see four more parties, candidates with friends and food. One party after the other enters the hut where *Kwarumba* remains hidden from curious eyes, and on his turn candidate *Zera* presents himself too. Entering with his friends, he seats himself opposite the woman in the pitch-dark hut and clicks his fingers against her, a gesture called *kasekwe male,* to ask the woman. Not one word will he speak, as his friends will plead his cause with the woman, saying, "Yesterday at the marketplace you said you loved *Zera.* Did you lie or do you still love him?" *Kwarumba,* who sits at ease with her youngest baby in a sling on her back, gives short affirmative answers: "Yes, I do love him." The men urge her to speak the truth, as no sane man will ever believe a woman who tells him that she loves him (and the same with a man professing his love to a woman). *Kwarumba* has to swear she loves *Zera.* His friends discuss the other candidates, among them *Vasekwa,* deemed the most dangerous competitor in this contest: "He, *Vasekwa,* has already a compound full of women: he would not even find you there." Asked about the *wume* that will have to be paid, *Kwarumba* say she does not care about a brideprice; she has four children now and can marry whomever she wants. *Zera Demu* and *Vasekwa* are her two favorite options.

> As all candidates have been in the hut, *TizhE* enters for a long talk with his kinswoman. Dusk is falling when she finally makes up her mind.

TizhE's wife appears to have had the biggest say in the matter; her candidate was *'Yite,* her brother, but *'Yite* did not want to marry *Kwarumba*
as he had a woman from Garta already and did not have that much
sorghum in his granaries (a new wife has to be well-fed) so he renounces
his candidacy in favor of his friend *Vasekwa.* So *Kwarumba's* choice
turns out to be *Vasekwa.* After sunset the other wives of *Vasekwa*
accompany her towards her new home; there, arriving at the entrance
hut, *Kwarumba* hesitates and has herself persuaded to enter the compound with some money (a standard procedure, as entering the house
is the actual wedding). Then she settles in an empty hut, built for a
former wife who has left. When a few days later a goat is slaughtered
(see below) she changes to her husband's hut as her own new hut is not
finished yet. But she actually never enters that one, as after a week
Kwarumba's brother comes to bring her back to her first husband in
Garta. She will never return to *Vasekwa* after her marriage of one week.

In this procedure the bride picks a husband she does not know at all, just as
the man may never have met her in full daylight.

The woman usually stays at least a week. On the third day after the

A young Kapsiki mother with her own and her friend's children.

wedding the bridegroom has his sister's son butcher a goat or sheep and present the parts to the following parties:

three paws and the chest	proxy father
skin of the head and larynx	the clan member who has given the goat, often the initiation father
heart, liver and part of the psalterium	husband's father
neck, part of the psalterium, tail, pancreas, large intestine	sister's son who has done the slaughtering
one kidney	daughter of husband
other kidney, half of the back	husband's mother
one paw	husband's sister
skull and rennet stomach	boy who has herded the goat

The rest of the meat is cut into small pieces and cooked. One of the friends prepares a special portion for the bride. He fills one of the stomachs with choice parts of meat and sews it shut with a piece of intestine and a few sticks after which he cooks the sack as a whole. At noon the food is ready and the old men of the ward assemble in the forecourt for the meal. Then *Kwatewume* is visited in her hut by the husband's friend, who presents her the cooked stomach with meat, urges her to eat, opens the sack and has her partake. When she starts eating, the elders in the forecourt eat their share too.

After sunset the sister's son and the friend bring the proxy father his portion of meat plus seven dishes of sorghum and an iron rod. He would be a very unusual *mekwe* if he did not try to wring a few extra gifts from the situation by stressing his own importance as a go-between for husband's and wife's father, but this is done in a loose and relaxed atmosphere.

The procedure of the *kwe yitu*, goat for the flight, is quite characteristic for all ceremonies pertaining to the secondary marriage. Such a meal is held again after a few weeks, the *kwe kwarha durhwu*, goat to start cooking. This meal ends the marginal period for the *kwatewume*, in which she is extremely well-fed and has slept in her husband's hut. It has been a period of hectic sexual activity, with lots of meat to eat and other showing off, such as the newly married woman grinding sorghum in the small hours of the night. Often a *kwatewume* takes off again after this period of relaxation, pleasant for its entertainment and absence of hard work, as no work on the fields nor any cooking is expected of her. She often returns to her previous husband, as the "holiday" is over, in fact more than half of all short marriages (less than one month) end this way. Back "home" the woman picks up her old marriage without very much ado and usually the man welcomes his wife with a chicken. Compared to the elaborate and costly feasts of the first marriage this is a simple welcome indeed.

Thus far we have given the picture from the point of view of the new husband. However, for every man gaining a wife, another is losing his. The bereaved husband may just sit tight and wait until his wife comes back or he may embark on a more active course. His father-in-law might be persuaded to retrieve his daughter, in which case often the wife's brother performs the task. His influence, as we shall see in the next chapter, is considerable. The wife's kin can go back and forth to the new village of the bride without any danger, as no one will harm his in-laws, be it his own or that of a co-villager. When her brother or father arrives, no woman resists them. This does not always imply that she will stay with her first husband. If she is stubborn she runs away again the following night:

> *Sunu Teri* married *KwayEngu* as a *kwatewume*. However, her father, *Kweji,* wanted her to stay with her first husband in Kamalé, who was a rich man and had paid a considerable brideprice not yet repaid in children. His relations with *Sunu* were strained, to say the least. After arriving at *Sunu's* compound *KwayEngu* permitted herself to be guided back to Kamalé after one week of marriage, but returned to Mogodé the the same night (a two-hour walk). The next morning, *Kweji* again took her to her *zamakwa,* but again in vain as he had to repeat the perform-ance in the afternoon. Both were stubborn, and *KwayEngu* commuted five times between Mogodé and Kamalé within one week. At last her perseverance won out, and she stayed with *Sunu.*

If no in-law is willing to go, the husband may send one of his wife's children to get her, or he himself may look for her. A child runs no risk going into a strange village, but for a man this last resort is by no means safe.

The village of a *zamale* is a very hostile environment, and the former husband sneaks in under the cover of the night to the village where he suspects his wife to have settled. A ritual ally or a maternal kinsman may help him locate the compound and to spot his wife. Hearing him she will come out to avoid difficulties and he can escort her home. Resisting would be shameful for her; in addition, she would not be able to claim much assistance as she is a stranger in the village herself. Formerly, if the daring husband was caught by his *zamale* he was in danger of a flogging or torture if he was not her *zamakwa* (see Chapter 1). Now peace reigns and more husbands venture into hostile villages, but it is still a risky business:

> *KwayEngu,* after three years of marriage, gave birth to a little boy. How-ever, *KwayEngu* did not become pregnant again, so when the boy was about five she left *Sunu* again for her first husband, *Deli,* in Kamalé. She stayed a year with him. On a rainy night in the wet season, she suddenly appeared in *Sunu's* home to ask if he would agree to her coming back. *Sunu* answered, "This is your house, there is your boy." She went back to Kamalé to get her things. As the days passed without her showing up, *Sunu* grew restless. At the time of the weeding of the

sorghum he descended to Kamalé, where he found his competitor busy taking sorghum from his granary. *Sunu* did not address him as it is very impolite to speak to someone who is inside his granary (it is taboo to speak inside a granary and, therefore, he could not answer). However, *Deli* saw him coming and started a brawl.

"Don't you believe I can take you to Michika anytime I want to (to be tried in court)," he said. Quick in taking offense like any Kapsiki, *Sunu* abused his *zamale* and challenged him to fight. *KwayEngu,* who had been grinding sorghum with her co-wives, heard the brawl and wanted to join *Sunu,* but *Deli* forced her back into her hut. At the last moment wisdom prevailed and *Sunu,* seeing he would not achieve anything worthwhile, returned home; when traveling to Kamalé, he had no clear idea what he wanted to accomplish anyway.

A few weeks later he heard from clansmen that *Deli* was going to Sir, where *KwayEngu's* father lived. Although he normally never walked armed, he took a stick and a knife with him and waited at several points on the route, but an older clansman took away the knife, while a mother's brother and a blacksmith friend tried to keep him from attacking his zamale. He suddenly saw *Deli* pass by on his way back to Kamalé. *Sunu* ran after the fleeing *Deli* and overtook him just on the border of the two villages. *Deli* started to scold him again, took off his gown and came towards *Sunu*, sword in hand. *Sunu* later told about this moment: "I did not know what to do, when suddenly I heard a *gutuli* (spirit) say 'count to five after he draws his sword.'" Thus he did. *Deli* struck four times but succeeded only in wounding *Sunu* with a near miss. Then *Sunu* struck *Deli* forcefully with his bludgeon, hitting him on the neck and felling him instantly. *Sunu* wanted to drag him towards the chief of Mogodé, but, forgetting to disarm him, he got a fierce gash in his right hand and had to let his victim go. He tried to overtake *Deli* again, but his *zamale* was terribly fast in fleeing and left his gown, an electric torch and 11.000 CFA behind. Of course *Sunu* gathered this unexpected harvest in, considering the 11.000 CFA a present for his *KwayEngu.* Back home in Kamalé *Deli* told everyone that he had been ambushed by at least five dacoits, and even if his people did not believe him wholly, people in both villages were convinced *Sunu* had some potent magic. *Deli* tried to get his things back and summoned *Sunu* to court in Kamalé. When *Sunu* admitted having the gown and the torch but denied any knowledge as to the 11.000 CFA, the Kamalé chief rendered judgment by calling for a rooster ordeal (an ordeal to choose between contending claims). *Sunu* bragged that he did not fear any ordeal, and would not even prepare himself for it (i.e., would seek no magic to support his cause), but *Deli* hesitated, as he had claimed the money to be 16.000 CFA instead of 11.000, and he cancelled the ordeal saying, "It is not sure, the money. Maybe it has fallen at the fight." *Sunu* even wanted to push his luck further by impeaching his *zamale*, but the chief justly prohibited this. All the while *KwayEngu* had still not returned to *Sunu's* compound. A few weeks after the conflict he consulted a shepherd of the chief who gave him magic to get her back. Despite his initial skepticism about it, it worked splendidly and after two days *KwayEngu* returned to him and to her boy, thoroughly pleased with the "war" the two men had waged over her.

Paying the Brideprice — and Getting It Back

As we have seen before, brideprice plays a vital role in social relations; in fact it provides the fulcrum for many inter- and intravillage processes. *Makwa* brideprices are paid over a long time, in fact over the many years leading up to the actual wedding and over all the years the union is going to last. The total *wume* (brideprice) consists of an amalgam of different sorts of gifts — money, goats, sheep, clothes, iron, soda, labor, etc.; the ultimate amount is not ascertained beforehand. Questions about a lump sum would be both unanswerable for a father-in-law, who envisages no "price" for his daughter, and shameful, as it would be too much like selling the bride.

Not being established in advance, the *wume* depends on a lot of factors: the length of the union, the wealth of the *zamakwa,* the perseverance of the father-in-law and, last but not least, the number of children born. Most *wume* total between 20.000 and 60.000 CFA ($70-200):

> The longest *makwa* union we found, *Kweji Medu* and his *makwa, KwanyE Zera*, has lasted 47 years (not counting the 7 months *KwanyE* had stayed at another husbands') and the *wume* amounted to: 30 goats, 4 legs of beef, 1 cow, 2 knolls of soda, 1 gown, 4 balls of tobacco, and buffalo and antelope meat.
> As a comparison the recent union of *Wazha* and *Kwarumba* amounted to: 6 goats, 15.000 CFA, 5 balls of tobacco 3 knolls of soda, and 3 legs of beef.

A good *wume* should contain traditional items such as tobacco, soda, iron rods and legs of beef. In modern marriages money is becoming more and more important, mostly replacing goats! Beer, jars and gifts of sorghum to the girl's parents, perfume and other small presents to the girl are not counted as *wume*; they are not refunded when the brideprice is restituted.

Any brideprice for the *makwa* as well as for the *kwatewume* is primarily a payment for the children, in fact a childprice. Whoever paid or will in the future pay the brideprice is entitled to all children. A child born is considered a restitution for that brideprice. The blessings given to the bride were explicit on this. In former days any birth, even stillbirths or miscarriages, repaid a *wume*. Enforced repayment of the *wume* lost its efficacy after blood had been shed. Today a fair number of repayments are done through the courts; in general, two children, living or dead, counterbalance the brideprice. This is typical African thinking; brideprice is repaid in two children. This rule, however, does not apply in the traditional Kapsiki system.

If a wife disappears leaving her first and only child behind, a man can reclaim in a lawsuit half of his money. However, this is rare, as by far the majority of brideprice refunds are processed the traditional way (see below):

> *TizhE Tange* had paid no money for *KwanyE,* a *kwatewume* he married years ago and who had given him several children already. When, after many years, the *zamakwa* of *KwanyE* despaired of having his *makwa* back and reclaimed his money and goats, *TizhE* was in trouble. He had neither cash nor beasts to reimburse the *zamakwa*, so he gave one of the children to the first husband. The child, a boy, grew up as that man's son and both men were quite content with the solution.

As we have seen before, paying the brideprice for a runaway woman heavily depends on the children born. Usually the woman's father or brother claims the first part of the eventual *wume* after the birth of the first child. Then the husband goes over to his in-laws' compound with a huge gift of white beer, called *mpedli kanjungwe mekwe* (just like the beer gift in the *makwa* rites), at which occasion he meets his father-in-law for the first time. The two men start their relationship, the father asking for money and goats, the husband trying to stall and diminish his gifts.

For each following child the procedure is repeated so the amount of the brideprice for a *kwatewume*—though it stays always inferior to the total amount of a *makwa* brideprice—closely corresponds to the number of children born from the union.

The process of gradual brideprice payment may be countered by one intervening factor: the previous husband may reclaim his brideprice if—of course—he has received no children. Although he will direct his claims to his father-in-law (even when his wife has left him, her father remains his *mekwe*—father-in-law) this *mekwe* invariably will charge the new husband. Usually any benefit gained from his daughter's marriage has long since disappeared, often in brideprice for his own new wives; anyway a daughter is a relation to gain money, not to spend it on. So the *mekwe* will charge the new husband at least the total amount of the former *wume*, a considerable sum in which the latter has to be helped by friends and kinsmen. In such cases the Kapsiki say, "He pays his *kwatewume* like a *makwa*"; i.e., in advance of any children born, and quite expensively too. If the new husband has some children, he might give a child to the first husband:

Zera Mpa married a woman from Roumsou, called *Kwashukwu,* who left her *zamakwa* immediately after the *makwa* rites. *Zera* knows her first husband is vengeful and can be expected to claim his money back. Two weeks after she moved into his compound, he carries the greeting gift of beer after the falling of dusk to his father-in-law, *Ndewuva,* who happens to be the headman of Roumsou village.

Ndewuva asks, "Why do you come at night?"
Sunu, Zera's friend, witness and spokesman answers, "That is the custom. Who are we to change the customs? If we came in full daylight, people would object." *(Zera* and *Sunu* are *zamale* of Roumsou; besides people do not like the daughters of their headmen to disappear to other villages).

Ndewuva: "Why did *Zera Mpa* brew beer? I need money, not beer. I fear the other one's magic only and *Zera Mpa* should alleviate this fear." Then he says how many goats and how much money he wants from *Zera,* and explains that he never asks too much for his daughters, save for one married to a schoolteacher, a Moslem who will never give anything anymore. After ascertaining whether *Kwashukwu* wants *Zera* as a husband, whether *Zera* can pay the amount and finally whether they sleep together, he continues:

"I won't take away your wife, have no fear. I married a girl from Mogodé myself. Just collect the *wume.* I know of nobody else to give her to. Her former husband's father has sworn she or any of her children will die if they enter his compound and I want my daughter to live."

The first husband was incensed because *Kwashukwu* refused to return to his house for the concluding *makwa* ritual during the oncoming annual festival, so he reclaimed all of his money. In this conversation *Ndewuva* asked for 30.000 CFA and eight goats. *Sunu* argues on *Zera's* behalf and the amount was reduced to 23.000, one cow of 6000 CFA and four goats. In this negotiation *Sunu* knows himself to be supported by *Kwashukwu's* mother who lives with one of their sons elsewhere in Roumsou. She so much wanted *Kwashukwu* to marry *Zera Mpa* that she offered one cow to help with the *wume.*

About a month later, after the *la* festival, the brideprice was paid very discreetly by *Zera's* friend, *Sunu,* with only *Zera,* his *mekwe, Sunu* and myself present:

Sunu: "Last time we talked about *Kwashukwu's* brideprice. It is a lot of money and we had to borrow all over the place to collect it. So here it is." He counts 20.000 CFA before *Ndewuva's* feet. However, his *mekwe* does not touch the money but retorts, "How can I take it? It is not complete. If all the money was here, I would take it, but this is insufficient. Now I cannot pay the first husband." After some more discussion *Zera* adds another 4000 CFA and *Ndewuva* takes it. The goats will follow; there is no more talk about the cow. Eyeing all his money,

Ndewuva asks whether his daughter is pregnant already. The answer is no. "God, she has to become pregnant soon; with all that money here and my daughter still not pregnant...."

Well, he should not have worried. In the next five years *Kwashukwu* did not leave *Zera Mpa* and gave him three healthy children, all of them daughters, so *Zera Mpa* is very pleased, expecting to become a rich man himself later.

In addition to the money given to *Ndewuve, Zera* gave 8000 CFA to *Kwashukwu's* brother and some 3500 CFA to her mother. Though the bride's father probably did not know about this, they were fully entitled to some gifts from *Zera*.

In this case we saw *Ndewuva* fear his daughter's first husband. As debtor *Ndewuva* is open to magical attack. As long as no price is refunded, any son-in-law who wants to force his claims places a bundle of so-called *sekwa* within his debtor's compound, and as a consequence all inhabitants will die "like an epidemic." When no debts are outstanding the *sekwa* has no power. A bridegroom should beware of becoming part and parcel of his *mekwe's* compound and should refuse any food cooked in it. He may drink beer brewed in his fiance's parental home as beer is social food, but if he partakes of mush or meat the *sekwa* will "follow" him too.

This *sekwa* is the main traditional means of extracting brideprice repayments: the amount of the debt is established by the witnesses who have assisted in all transactions between the two parties. Formerly grass stalks were used to remember the gifts: noded stalks for goats or sheep, stalks without nodes for rams or billy-goats, a twig for a cow, a flattened stalk and a cloth-wrapped twig for meat and clothes respectively.

In our case *Ndewuva* tried to get some personal gain, a common and respected goal for any *mekwe*. In such transactions, with a daughter leaving without giving birth, he has several options. His main chance is that the former husband will not reclaim his *wume*. Reasons for this are divers: it is shameful to ask too quickly for a refund and most men get quite a kick out of "commanding" a *makwa;* i.e., perpetuating their rights over the woman and/or children. If the former husband has any hope that his *makwa* will return to him, he will prefer to leave the brideprice at his *mekwe's*. The critical point usually is when the woman gives birth to a living child from her new husband. The former husband then despairs of having her back since a woman usually stays with a husband who gives her children. Then he will reclaim his money. On the whole the reasons for leaving the *wume* unclaimed prevail and about 50% of all reclaimable brideprice is never in fact reclaimed, comprising a considerable gain for the girl's father.

Other means of gaining extra are by charging a little surplus from the next husband (as *Ndewuva* did in the above-mentioned case) or by separating both transactions, payment and repayment, in order to manipulate several conflicting claims. The father of a girl routinely tries to maximize his

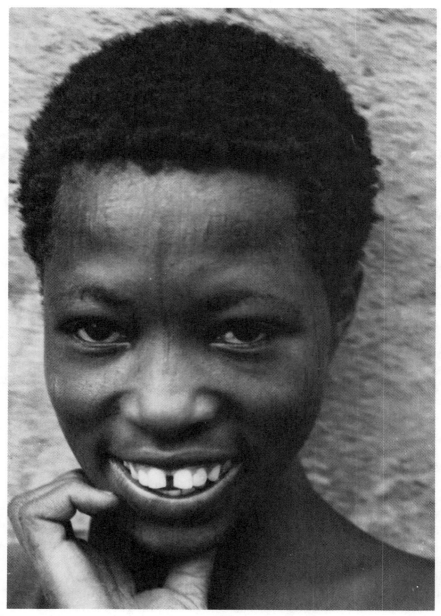

Kwashukwu

benefits by accepting gifts for his daughters from any candidate; he similarly tries to stall or to dodge a refund by confronting claimants with each other:

> The same *Zera Mpa* who paid the brideprice for *Kwashukwu* in the example above also married a Mogodé girl, *Kwangwushi*, a *makwa* who left her first husband immediately after the rites. Her father *Teri Di* was no stranger in the brideprice business and was himself entangled in a complex web of debt relations. *'Yama*, his daughter's *zamakwa*, had given him 16000 CFA thus far, but in the same preparatory period *Teri Di* had acquired some 12000 CFA from another would-be-husband while *Zera* had given 8000 CFA to pose his candidacy. The moment *Kwangwushi* leaves *'Yama* to head home, her father's life becomes quite exciting. The *zamakwa* and the other candidates beleaguer him for his daughter. *Teri Di* then quickly comes to an agreement with *Zera Mpa*, implying that his daughter will come to *Zera*. To let him save face however, and in order to furnish *Teri Di* with room for negotiations with the other candidates, he will pretend to know nothing about it. And so it happens. In the small hours of the night two friends of *Zera* sneak into the parental compound and convince *Kwangwushi* to come with them. After some hesitation, partly due to the heavy rains pouring down inter-mingled with fiery flashes of lightning and partly due to customary reti-cence of a bride, *Kwangwushi* joins the two soaking wet men and briskly trots the two-hour walk toward *Zera's* compound. There she enters in the usual manner of a *kwatewume* and does not appear in public for some weeks. *Teri* pretends not to know of his daughter's whereabouts, and it takes the *zamakwa* *'Yama* several weeks to locate his ex-bride; in that period the conviction that *Kwangwushi* will not return to him slowly grows. A month after this development *'Yama* reclaims his money through his witness.
>
> However, claiming the brideprice is far easier than actually getting the money back, especially with a practical and shrewd father-in-law like *Teri Di*. The latter arranges the negotiations over *'Yama's wume* in an unusual manner—a public discussion between the two parties is arranged, with the new husband present. Although customarily all *wume* transactions are performed privately and both husbands never meet each other, *Teri Di* deems it useful to associate the two operations. Establishing the total amount of the *wume* paid by *'Yama* takes no less than three hours of fervent discussion. Any *makwa* brideprice consists of a huge number of small and varied gifts given at different times, often with different witnesses for each presentation. All these gifts are depicted in full with all relevant and redundant details (on what occasion, what time and by whom the gift had been presented, who were the witnesses and so on). All gifts are indicated through traces in the sand, as the *wume* will have to be refunded goat for goat, franc for franc and (Nigerian) pound for pound. Gifts of tobacco and meat are

not to be refunded in kind but in cash as established after a lengthy and obstinate debate. The dispute grows heated as *'Yama*, embittered because his ex-bride remarried within the same village, truly wants his pound of flesh. He refuses the goats *Zera Mpa* presents, claiming his goats were far superior to anything *Zera* could ever dream of, and also—a far more unusual claim—even asks back clothes, soda, perfume and beer jars. Although an agreement on the "normal" brideprice had been reached, this countercustomary claim enrages *Teri Di* and the whole matter has to be settled in court.

After two weeks the canton chief renders judgment: *Teri Di* has to refund 16000 CFA, 5 Nigerian pounds, 10 shilling, 2 legs of meat and 16 goats, almost the precise sum agreed upon before. No perfume, clothes, beer or jars are to be repaid as these items are considered to be normal expenses for posing one's candidacy and never constitute an integral part of the *wume*. *'Yama* gets a reprimand for being greedy. Although *Teri Di* is rebuked by the chief for letting that many men pay on the same girl, he evades repaying several gifts. In fact, he gains enough money to marry a wife himself. *Zera Mpa*, although well-aware he has paid a lot more than *'Yama* through this intricate procedure, did appreciate his father-in-law's dexterity in handling this bridal business. "A good *mekwe*," he said.

Although *Teri Di* got away with his dealings, not all fathers are that deft. Conflicting claims or uncautious promises can create serious problems for a *mekwe*. He may have pocketed money from several prospective new spouses. When they do reclaim it—as the daughter can choose only one—he is in trouble. The money usually has been spent on a new wife for himself, and the new husband is seldom willing to pay that much extra.

All these complicated debt relationships occur only when the woman bears no children (or in the modern situation less than two children). When children have "repaid" the brideprice no debt remains. To the contrary, the son-in-law stays in the debt of his father-in-law, as life never can be paid fully. So a fertile daughter is a sure gain for her father. When she has borne two or three children her father will put some pressure on her to look for another husband. The present one cannot be expected to give any more substantial gifts, so only a new husband can bring some benefit. Although a father may command a change in marriage, his influence is limited. He can neither direct his daughter towards a specific new husband, nor can he prevent her returning to her previous mate, which often happens as women tend to return to their children. In her choice of a spouse, the woman may be bolstered by her mother's brother, who will usually endorse the preference of his sister's daughter, or by her own brother, with whom she often has a good and intimate relationship.

With the passage of time the woman gets more and more independent in her marital career; her father's influence lessens and after his death her brothers, who fill his social niche, have neither the authority nor the will to thwart their sister's wishes.

Marriage Frequency

Kapsiki marriage is extremely brittle. Although in other tribes in the Mandara region a high marital instability is reported too, (Vincent 1972, Martin 1970, Pontie 1973, Fuillerat 1971, Podlewski 1966, Richard 1977), the Kapsiki are the most unstable. The average Kapsiki man has had 8.5 wives and a wife has had 4 husbands. A Kapsiki man of about 42 years of age is perhaps married to one or two women, while 7 other wives have already left his compound. The average Kapsiki woman, aged about 36 years, has passed through three husbands (and villages!) and resides with her fourth.

The divorce ratio is very high: less than 4% of all marriages are ended by the death of one partner! The mean marriage expectancy is accordingly low: a Kapsiki man or woman at the brink of a new marriage can expect to stay married with that partner 4.2 years. Of all 100 marriages, 50% end after 12 months.

Considering the differences between the two marriage types, *makwa* and *kwatewume*, one would rightfully expect a difference in mean marriage duration.

Table 5: Mean Marriage Expectancy per Marriage Type

	mean	median
makwa	9.4 y.	5y.
kwatewume	3.0 y.	7 months
widow inheritance	3.2 y.	2.5 y.
stolen *makwa*	21 days	10 days
Total	4.2 y.	1.1 y.

These data solve one persistent question that vexed us during our research. Why should a man go through that much trouble, take that many risks and make such strenuous efforts to marry a girl who will inevitably leave him? The figures of Table 6 indicate that this work and these gifts do form a reasonable investment for a man as they make for a fair return in married years and in chances for children. A *makwa* stays longer and—as we shall see below—is more fertile than a runaway woman. In contrast, stealing a *makwa*—the marriage with a *derheli*—seldom proves successful. In the majority of *makwa* "thefts," the bride is returned by her parents to her original bridegroom within a few weeks. Widow inheritance has the same mean expectancy as the *kwatewume* marriage, but far fewer short marriages occur. The most important factor in marriage frequency (it is difficult to speak of divorce frequency in the Kapsiki setting) is the huge amount of exceptionally short *kwatewume* marriages: 50% are terminated after seven months. Only the rare unions which last for years make for a reasonable average duration. The distribution is heavily skewed toward the shorter marriages.

Even if one marriage type is relatively more stable than another, any genre of Kapsiki marriage is brittle. In fact, marriage is at best a temporary union between two persons. This fragility originates in the mobility of the woman. This high mobility is due to several factors. First there is the fragmentation and atomization of Kapsiki social organization, preventing the formation of larger corporate groups which might be able to curtail mobility. Often in African societies a marriage means a liaison between two corporate groups. In this society, composed of autonomous minimal agnatic groups, each claiming and sustaining its cherished autarchy, a marital union hardly provides a link between those small agnatic groups. The women themselves, instrumental in these relations as they may be, pursue their own independent course as they are never tied permanently to any husband or village, relying on their own sources of cash income and on matrilateral kin for their social network.

As we have seen, children are the main raison d'être for a marriage and the same holds for marital stability. Though the mobility of the women has eroded mother-child relations, living children are among the most important factors for marital stability. Without living progeny, be it caused by sterility or by the exceptionally high infant mortality in Kapsiki society, female mobility is at its peak. As both sterility and death of children are blamed on the husband or his village, a new husband and a new village should be sought.

The more marriages she contracts, the less fertile a woman is, and — of course — vice versa. A *makwa* is a man's best chance of having children, an often married woman the worst.

Above, we pointed out some general factors enhancing mobility. What do informants state on this issue? For many of them, in any case for most men, these women on the move constitute a real problem. Women, too, are well aware of their role in this complex of social relations. They are the party taking the initiative for marital change; they should be asked for motives first. In fact, no sane man ever banishes a wife from his compound. Someone may neglect a wife, inducing her to depart, but this is very exceptional. The women give a number of reasons, not for their mobility but for leaving one specific husband to remarry elsewhere. The reasons can be categorized into four general groups:

1. No explicit reason or inducement for leaving;
2. Problems in the husband's compound;
3. Influence of her father;
4. Sterility or infant mortality.

Group 1: A substantial number of women said that they left a particular husband "just for nothing," without any reason at all. A strong tradition for habitually changing marital ties shows from expressions such as: "I do not leave myself; my feet simply walk away" or "Do you know, we women just walk from village to village." The women of a ward ridicule a sister who has never left her husband, never visited another village. Some women publicly state they have married their present husband *"KazhEne mpi"* to rest a while for a little vacation, saying so even in the presence of their not-so-appreciative husband. The duration of the marriage is no factor in this whatsoever. Many a woman looks at her husband after, say, 15 years of marriage, decides she does not love him anymore and simply walks away, leaving behind any children she may have born.

Group 2: The husband is often blamed by the women if problems abound in the compound. Either he does not give her enough sorghum to cook or he takes her possessions; he beats her too hard or deprives her sexually. He may be too old, too small; he may turn Christian or Muslim, or he may move to another place in the village. Any of these reasons may be sufficient for a wife to leave him.

Other problems originate from co-wives, but quite ambiguously. Their absence can be a nuisance since all household chores will be done alone. However, jealousy can exist between competing co-wives. In the same way, the husband's mother may be a factor; she can be very annoying. A fair number of women actually prefer having her on the premises as an ameliorating factor in the husband-wife relationship.

Group 3: The woman's patrilineal line, especially her father and brothers, can be an inducement to change. In fact, quite a number of women mention this influence, either in running away from or in returning to their husbands.

Group 4: Sterility and infant mortality, as we have seen, are of utmost importance in breaking marriage ties. A woman does not remain in the location where her children die. Kapsiki demography is characterized by an exceptionally high infant mortality in which only 334 infants per 1000 born reach the age of 5 (Podlewski 1966). The causes for this dramatic mortality are tied closely to the marital mobility of the mothers. As women leave, they leave their children behind with their father. If these children are still very young, just after weaning, their chances for survival become much smaller. One can see them sulking, feeling dejected and lost. Other wives of their father will care for them less than for their own offspring. Less-fed and psychologically hurt, these children tend to fade away gradually. Children die from "natural causes" too, especially from malaria, dysentery and the fierce epidemics of meningitis that yearly ravage the mountain area. As children die, women leave again, blaming the death on their husband's village. Thus child mortality and women's mobility create positive feedback on each other (van Beek 1986a).

The reasons men state for their wives' departure are on the whole less pertinent, but show clearly the relationship between the two sexes. According to most men, the wife left without any reason at all: "Women roam the country like grasshoppers," "their feet are used to walking the roads" or "nothing was the matter; she went to fetch water and never came back," or "she just liked to taste some meat (in fact some women mentioned this too!)." If any reason should be found, the woman is to blame: she was lazy, stupid, stubborn, objected to grinding white sorghum (a hard-grained variety). Jealousy between co-wives is perceived by the men too. A few men said they were willfully neglectful because their wives cohabitated with too many men or because they turned out to be witches.

The Rise and Decline of the Married State

The high marriage frequency has very serious repercussions on Kapsiki social life. In the concluding section we shall explore the consequences for the relationships between men and women. Here we shall dwell on the influence on the individual life histories of Kapsiki men and women.

Following their marital histories, two categories of women may be discerned: those women who return from time to time to their *zamakwa* and those who lose contact with their first husband altogether.

A woman of the first type has one long marriage, interrupted by a number of shorter unions, often with just a few different husbands! The second type of marital history occurs when a woman does not return to her first husband; she normally will make a tour over the various Kapsiki villages and lose contact with her native place. We shall give an example of both types:

> *Kweji TizhE,* a Mogodé-born woman of about 50, married *Bere* of Mogodé when she was 15 years of age. After eleven years of marriage, during which five children were born, she left *Bere* for *'Yamte* in Roumsou. After one month in his compound she returned to *Bere.* Two years later she disappeared to *Kweji RhwE* in Kamalé, where she stayed for two years. Back again to *Bere,* and the next year off to Sena, to *TizhE Derha.* She remained three years with *TizhE* followed by six months at *Bere's* and another stay of one and a half years with *TizhE*

again. In her 45th year she returned to *Bere* and stayed with him ever since. She has children in the compound of both *Bere* and *TizhE,* and so might be expected to continue to commute between those two husbands.

Kuve Teri, a woman of 29 years, married at the age of 15. *Teri Mte* was her *zamakwa* in her native village of Mogodé. After two years of marriage and one baby girl, her father told her to leave *Teri. Kuve* chose Kamalé, and found *Cimeha* as a husband in whose compound she stayed for three years and bore one child. However, *Cimeha* paid almost no brideprice so she left taking her two young children with her. The village of Kilu was to be her next stop. She married a man called *Teri* (a different one) but a week after joining his household her youngest child died, so she left immediately, now for nearby Garta. Both children seemed to have caught the same illness and after 15 days in Garta, implying 15 days of marriage of course, the other child died. *Kuve* went off to Sena where she took up house with *Sunu Dzale* after a ten-day "excursion" to a certain *TizhE Meha* in Futu. Her next four years proved more restful; she stayed in Sena with *Sunu* and gave birth to two children. A hectic quarrel forced her out of his house and at that time she went back to Mogodé, her village of origin, to marry *Zera Teri Beja* (not her *zamakwa,* who was still about). Four years of marriage, during which one daughter was born, led up to the present date. So, motivated by paternal urgings and infant mortality she made quite a marital journey.

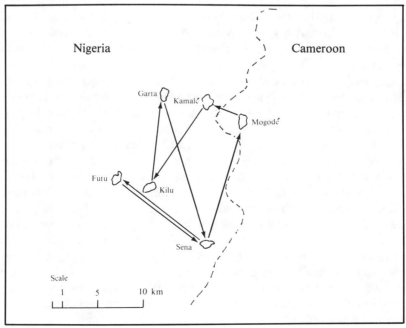

In both instances, whether a woman returns to her *zamakwa* or not, in her last living years she usually will not remain with any husband. As the average difference in married age between men and women is about 8 years, husbands tend to die before their wives. Instead of remarrying, many aged widows prefer to spend their declining years with a son, if possible a son in her native village. Even before her husband's death she may do the same; after menopause she leaves her husband, never to remarry, but to take up home with a son of hers. As she has taken no other husband, she remains the wife of the husband she left, but after the passage of time her marital status becomes progressively indistinct, and at any rate socially irrelevant. Living in her native village she often visits her brothers as their affectionate sister, but her main concern is her son. An intimate and easy relationship with him prevails and more often than not she is on good terms with his wife or wives. Over the years the old lady may have accumulated a considerable capital in cattle or goats which she puts at her son's disposal in order to marry new wives. Her other kin are not forgotten. Daughters who live dispersed over the neighboring villages, are visited at regular intervals, after the birth of a baby or on other important occasions. At the initiation or marriage rites of a descendant she plays a vital role, and on the whole she follows closely the lives of her kinsmen. Having a first hand knowledge of neighboring villages and a detailed knowledge of her kith and kin living over there, such an old woman is often a local authority on kinship relations outside the village.

Women do not always search for a new husband. Leaving the old one on their own initiative, they sometimes settle independently—neither with their kinsmen nor with a new spouse. The Kapsiki use the term "widow" for these women, a term they translate into French as "free woman." When they go to the cities, such as Mokolo (Cameroon), Michika or Maiduguri (Nigeria) they almost exclusively have to rely on prostitution, if they do not marry a husband. In the villages these women depend on subsistence cultivation of millet and sorghum and on small-scale peanut cultivation, which they supplement by some prostitution. Every activity takes place in the season most suited for it: cultivation is taken up in the rainy season; men have money and leisure to spend on these free women in the dry season. In the Kapsiki area these women are most numerous in either Mogodé as the cantonal siege with its numerous Islamized Kapsiki, or in Rhumsiki where tourists provide additional clientele. However, in both instances, the free women are not restricted to the modernizing villages or towns, nor is their occurrence a result of Islamization or tourism. This inclination of women to settle down independently is, in fact, quite traditional. Formerly such a situation arose when a woman had reached menopause, preferred not to stay with her husband and went to live on her own. Now they have the means to settle down at an earlier age, without being *de facto* a widow:

Gauwa, a woman of Rhumsiki, left her husband after six years of marriage. Both her children had died in infancy and she had constant quarrels with her husband. She joined her brother in Mokolo, but when he forced her to marry a Muslim, she left town again. "I went for a stroll to see life for a few days, but it turned out to be seven years." In that time she lived in the Nigerian city of Maiduguri, mainly from prostitution. A quarrel with another woman over a man forced her out. At the time, Nigeria ousted all foreign immigrants. Looking for a place to stay she asked her Rhumsiki kinsmen to let her have some fields to till and a place to build her hut. As always, this was granted without any problem, so she has been living for the last few years as a free woman in Rhumsiki.

For Kapsiki society this arrangement does not bear any stigma whatsoever. Young and older men habitually resort to the services of these women. They may be prominent in any organization of women in the village. The women selling at the market, for example, are organized in a loose conglomerate. One "chief of the market" sets norms for prices of beer, as well as of other products. Such a women's chief often is a free woman.

The consequences of this "marriage complex" show most clearly with the men. The mobility of a wife presents an enduring threat to marital status and a Kapsiki is very conscious of it. Women, marriage and all matters pertaining to the peopling of their household form recurrent topics in everyday conversation. Marrying a wife calls for some hard labor but staying married is harder still: one has to keep marrying new women lest one become a bachelor again. In our portrait of a real *za* (man) we state that he should dance every few years in the village festival (see Chapter 6). The more polygynous one is, the more attentive one should be:

YEngu Dzale is one of the richest men in Mogodé, perhaps not in worldly goods but certainly in people. At the time of our marriage survey he was married to 10 women. They all lived together with their 21 children in the same compound, a vast complex of interconnected huts, kitchens and granaries. Strangers like us had a hard time discovering the single entry in the enormous wall. About eight months later, at the time we had to leave, four of his women had left him. However, he had married two *kwatewume*, conducted negotiations with a woman in Sena to join him and was busy with preparations for marrying a *makwa* next season.

Like the individual women, a Kapsiki man has a very turbulent marital history. His compound, although a permanent residence for himself, often turns out to be just a way station for the women entering his door in marriage, thus changing the composition of his household constantly. However, men are not created equal. One easily perceives a fair difference between the "haves" and the "have-nots" in the marital domain. A few typical cases may illustrate these discrepancies. In the average life history of a Kapsiki man two periods are characterized by a hectic marital life. The first one falls between his 20th and 27th year. In these years most young men marry their *makwa*. A young man then still lives in his father's compound, who helps him out with brideprice and wedding expenses, at least for his first *makwa*. Often the young man has tried to marry either a *kwatewume* or a young girl (stolen *makwa*) before this time, but more often than not in vain. After his first *makwa* marriage a number of *kwatewume* marriages follow in rapid succession, but again of short duration. During the next seven years the young man settles in his own compound, with his one or two wives and their children. He has some debts to pay off and spends his time building huts, kitchens and granaries in his compound and cultivating a lot. He also tries his luck in commerce.

It is in the third phase of his marriage life when he is 34-50 years old, that he has developed into a real *za*, a lord of the mansion. He is settled now, can marry more wives and is at the zenith of his social and marital life. *Makwa* as well as *kwatewume* enter into marriage with him. Although the young girls leave him quicker than before in search for a younger husband, the *kwatewume* stay longer in his house. Also, his chances to inherit a widow mount with the years. In this period his compound is at its largest: new huts for women, kitchens, etc., make up for a gradual increase in living space. New wives coming in take the empty huts of women that have left. This continuous labor force means a peak in the productive activities too: never before has the man "commanded" that much corn and sorghum, never before was his flock of cattle, sheep and goats that big.

Figure 7: Marital Histories of Four Men

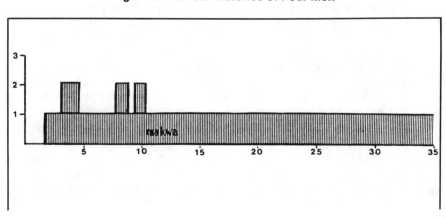

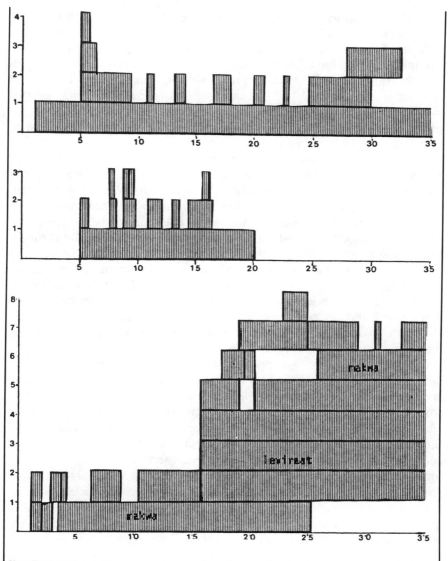

Key: Each horizontal bar represents a marriage; interruptions by absences are not marked. The total number of wives in the compound at a given age of the man is represented by an accumulation of bars. The man's age is indicated horizontally, counting the years after his initiation.

The first example presents a "monogamous" husband. His one and only *makwa* stayed with him and he did not marry many others, only three women who left soon. The second one, also a monogamous husband, offers a well-known pattern. The man did his utmost to become polygynous but to no avail; all those wives left him, some after several years of marriage, some very quickly. Number three is a poor man, a *rhwemzhi* (bachelor), a pitiable miser who has to perform his own household chores. No one can say he did not try, but all women have left him. Newly arriving women will eye him suspiciously: "What is wrong with that man?" and beware of entering his compound. The last case presents an important man of the village, a real *za*. He has labored constantly to marry as many wives as possible and is well off with his 6 women from 20 marriages. His women prove fertile, thus they do not leave him quickly.

Keeping the house full and the labor force up is a constant source of worry and action for the man. To stand still is to decline. However, after passing 50 he becomes less successful in his endeavors. Women depart, the young ones in search of a younger husband, the older ones heading for their sons. Often one woman remains with the old man, but sometimes none. He still commands some capital earned through his wives' labor and through his daughters' marriages, to use for his sons' brideprices and weddings. Although he himself is not overly active any more in the marital circuit, he is an important man among the village elders, especially if he has had many children. In discussions, beer parties and sacrificial ceremonies his voice is often heard and his advice heeded. Seated at the place of honor in the forecourt of any house, he freely administers his wise counsel to the listening younger men.

However, when old age prevents his social visits and impedes his mobility, the old man becomes a relic, an old man living alone in a huge compound crammed with empty huts. He then often comes to live in his son's compound, the son taking the social position of his father. He hardly leaves the compound and is forgotten by the village, sometimes long before his death. That is life's course for an important man. However, not all men succeed in consolidating their compound in the second marital period. Less lucky ones, less blessed with goods, have to make do with only one wife. Quite a few are even less fortunate and stay or become bachelors. The ratio of married men to married women is 1:1.6. With an age difference of 8 years, a number of men must be without wives. They have a hard time. In addition to all the time-consuming household chores, they have to look after their own daily subsistence. Their former wife or wives may have left one or more children with them, and they have to be cared for, too. If those bachelors have no kin to help them out—and several of them have few kinsmen to rely upon in addition to the stigma of being a poor relative— they are caught in a positive feedback loop: having to care for their children and for themselves they miss time to cultivate any surplus. Without a granary they can marry no *kwatewume*, let alone a *makwa*, and any wife entering their compound will quickly leave them again, either at her father's urgings or because the husband cannot furnish her with the bare necessities of life.

So the marriage complex hits different men in very different ways, making for a clear division between, as we have said, "haves" and "have-nots."

Husband and Wife

As men and women have different, even contrasting interests in life, a marked antagonism characterizes the relationship between the sexes. All contradictory obligations and interests—mobility versus a settled life, temporary bonds in floating relationships versus inherent group membership—hamper a lasting and intimate relationship between husband and wife.

This antagonism shows itself in several ways, one of them being a tendency to trick the partner. Many informants repeatedly state that a good relationship with any wife calls for *ntsehwele*, trickery, as one has to be cunning in dealing with a wife. Without trickery no marriage will last, so a stupid husband will always have an empty compound. Tricking the wife starts in the *makwa* rituals, when the girl and her companion have to be coaxed into the compound without too much expense. Any promises made to *makwa* are just words and their fulfillment is pure chance. Also a *kwatewume* who asks for money before entering the new husband's compound has to be talked into the house:

> When *Kwangwushi,* who was "stolen" from her father's house with his consent, arrived in *Zera Mpa's* compound, she asked for money as a persuasion to enter the house. *Zera Mpa* answered that he had payed a huge brideprice and was broke. "What did she want then?" She was persuaded to enter but asked 1000 CFA for *Zera's* first night with her and 500 CFA as an inducement to eat. Hearing that, *Zera Mpa* was livid, and he let her sleep alone for two nights. Afterwards his friend and witness, *Sunu,* taught him a lesson in dealing with wives: "You have done a bad thing. No good to have a new wife spend the night alone. It is much better to lie to her. What? She had pocketed 7000 CFA from you to refund a gift from another candidate. You should have said that she could keep 1500 CFA from this money. And later on you could take the whole 7000 by force, as it would stay your money."

So lying is a noble art between husband and wife, and women are as adept at it as men. When a woman picks her new spouse, she gives all kinds of promises to keep candidates on the string; each and every potential husband will hear that she loves him, even if she has never seen him before or if she does not even consider marrying him. The above-mentioned case provided an example in this; when the husband tried to regain the money, she held him at bay with all sorts of promises, pretenses and ruses till he just gave up hope and let her keep the money:

> After the brideprice of *Kwangwushi* (see above) had been paid, jealousy entered *Zera's* household, as the new wife still slept in *Zera's* hut, her own not being finished yet. As *Zera* was too short of cash to buy a new door to finish the hut, his other two wives offered to pay for it, 200 CFA each, in order to normalize the marital situation. *Zera* agreed, had to agree in fact, and bought the door. He installed *Kangwushi* in her new hut but when he tried to collect the promised 400 CFA his troubles started. His two wives evaded payment by any means. If he came at night, they said, "It is very well-hidden so I cannot find it in the dark," but when he asked them in full daylight they would not get it for fear he would see the place where they hid their money.

One intriguing method of opposition is "doubting each other": one partner doubts the statements of the other one, evoking a fierce verbal reaction in which both swear heavy oaths, sometimes in the form of betting, or conditional curses:

> Once upon a time there were a husband and wife. "I shall *'YE* (educate) you" they told each other. When the woman ground sorghum, she smeared the calabash to take grain from the granary with very slippery hibiscus. Then she told her husband, "Go and get some sorghum to grind for me. But do not break the calabash, for if you do, you have to repair it with the hairs from a young lion's tail." "All right," said the man. He went to the granary, took the calabash and let it slip from his fingers breaking it on the floor. So he had to obtain the hair from a lion's tail. (The story is too long to recite here in full. It tells how the man made friends with the lion's mother and after an eventful quest obtained the hairs and sewed up the calabash). Then he said, "Now it is my turn." He caught a pigeon and put it among the chickens. "If my chicken gets lost, you have to catch it for me: I can recognize it by its colors," he told his wife. Curious as she was, she looked in the chicken coop and the pigeon flew out. She went after it to search, but every time she returned with a bird, it turned out to be the wrong one. Six long years she roamed the bush until her face grew long with age. At last she gave up; so the husband won.

The word *'YE* is important here. It means "to educate," or "teaching manners," implying that one should make the other one's life difficult in order to prove one's point.

A husband may give his wives new names to denote their relationship. In these names the antagonism shows again, as they often express a profound distrust for the woman and the instability of their marriage:

> After paying the brideprice for *Kwangwushi, Zera Mpa* called his last wife *Wusukzevena* (I stand with empty hands) as the *wume* had totally depleted his resources. His first wife, *Kwampa,* was called *Kwetekwete* by him (loves the one, loves the other), as she had left him, returned again, and in fact was expected to leave again. She did.

Of course the women rally to his battle cry. When she is angry or feeling dejected, a woman tells her husband she might become a *male kwesere,* a wife of the morning (who leaves in the afternoon).

The antagonism between the sexes is expressed in a great many traditional stories, directly or indirectly. Quasi-Freudian motives such as castration of the husband by his wife, exchange of genitals and aggression against the vagina abound, intermingled with stories as cited above, in which man and woman engage in open combat.

In daily life the social worlds of both sexes are well-separated, not by any kind of purdah restriction, as women move about freely, but because women communicate with women, and men with men. Scarce are the communications between husband and wife during the day. For the women, a good co-wife, husband's mother or a friendly neighbor offer a great deal more companionship than any husband can ever give. Men walk about with friends and neighbors. Most cross-sex communications occur outside the marital union, between men and wives of other men. Although friendship between a man and woman is possible, the suspicion of marriage looms too large to make it an easy relationship. Yet Kapsiki like to play with fire, so the conversations between men and women often tend to challenge each other to cross the line. Countless are the oaths that are sworn between them, but the breaches of these are just as countless. As everyone realizes the futility of oaths between people intent on tricking each other, one tries to have the other swear on a special place in the bush where many *gutuli* (ghosts) live. These ghosts "follow" the breaker of oaths, thus sanctioning the oath. Nevertheless oaths are sworn and broken.

Despite the privacy that characterizes the compound, quarrels between husband and wife easily attract the attention of neighbors who can be expected to interfere. Both partners yell at each other without lowering their voices and many quarrels are settled by a third party. If not, they quickly escalate into beating, the husband beating the wife or vice versa. Women sense their own importance too much to sustain harsh treatment without any fuss:

One morning one of the ward elders could not greet in a normal fashion (by raising the right fist) because his hand was swollen. He had had a quarrel with his wife. Both had drunk a lot of beer, and then she had given an inappropriate response to a question from his side (how and what was impossible to ascertain). He had beaten her on the back with a stick, but she had retaliated in like manner on his hand. When he visited us one and a half hours later, the quarrel was over but the swelling lasted much longer.

When the quarrels reach that level of intensity, the marriage will be terminated as the marital tie cannot stand such a severe strain. The easy oaths sworn at the start of marriage life now turn into vows never to see each other again. However, time may soften anything, even the effects of these brawls, so after new problems with her next husband a woman may think of the child she left behind, and re-evaluate her former marriage. If she decides to return, a small ritual has to be performed to alleviate the oath. The husband kills a chicken and the wife cooks it. Both chew a twig of *mapa* (a tree), eat the larynx of the chicken saying *"shala* (god), sorry for the stupid things we have said." Both of them drink red beer and some ward members who have been invited drink too and finish the chicken.

Other problems besides the direct antagonism between male and female may endanger the social life of the household and may relate to the marriage problems in a more indirect way. One of these is the fact that many children have to be reared by a woman who is not their real mother. When such a woman has her own child too, she may neglect the former co-wife's child. Her ties to her own children are stronger than those binding her to her husband's offspring. Many stories relate to this danger; brothers warn each other against a woman coming into the village to marry: "Do not marry her for she has come to harm your children." One example of such a story tells about a woman coming in with a blind son who does not want to drink milk. Although the younger brother warns his elder one not to marry her, the latter cannot resist the temptation. The woman then clips out the eyes of another son of his, gives them to her own child and disappears. Now it is up to the younger brother, always the most intelligent one and the hero of these stories, to arrange matters.

The problem is, of course, tied in with polygyny. Many women like to have a co-wife on the premises as it gives them some companionship, makes the daily chores easier and less tedious and also heightens the status of her husband. A *merete,* co-wife, can be a good friend, an intimate companion if of the same age, or someone who teaches a young wife the facts of life if she is older. Several crafts such as pottery, medicine and basket weaving are often taught by co-wives. As we have seen, the absence of women can be a serious handicap for a man in obtaining a wife. In several instances, a

Women take care of each other's feet.

woman who left her husband returned to him after he married another wife.

Yet polygamy also creates its problems, especially *dlE*, jealousy, between the co-wives for the husband's favors. The slight preference *Zera* had for his third wife had been compensated at first by the fact that the brideprice was not paid yet, but after payment the other wives insisted on equal treatment. Of course, problems between women may also relate to the children the co-wives leave behind. Anyway, despite the rule that a man should treat his wives equally, the heart—as the Kapsiki say—cannot be forced. So within the household the family may be cleft along the lines of *kwajiweni* and *kwazerema,* preferred wife and not-loved wife, respectively. *Kwajiweni*, of course, is a covert "position" in the household. The only overt special situation of a wife is the husband's *makwa* if she is still present. A *kwajiweni* spends most nights with the husband (the rule is that wives take turns in cooking for and sleeping with the husband); she gets the most meat while her children have the best clothes and are well-fed. The other women are *kwazerema* and they have a far more difficult life—fewer clothes, less meat and less attention—easily causing jealousy. In traditional stories this *kwajiweni—kwazerema* division surfaces far more explicitly than in actual life; as always in these stories it is the social inferior who wins, so the *kwazerema* proves to be the only one who really loves her husband and whose children help their father. In daily life wives are shy of showing affection to, or of trying to care overtly for their husband, lest the co-wife accuses her of hoping to become *kwajiweni:*

> *Zera Mpa* came home from a funeral dance in nearby Kamalé. Thirsty from the long and steep climb, he called his wives to bring him water, but none appeared. Growing angry he beat them until his older neighbor (and clansman) intervened, arguing: "They just looked at each other, to see what the other would do — whether she wanted to become *kwajiweni* or not."

To avoid these problems, Kapsiki men believe, one should have an even number of wives: a pair more easily become friends while a third one invites jealousy.

It is clear that the total "costs" of the marriage system with its inherent instability are considerable. Life histories of both men and women are dominated by it, care of children is endangered and the relationship between husband and wife is severely damaged. All interhuman relations are permeated by a sense of insecurity, distrust of the partner leading to an ultimate loneliness of the individual, or in the words of the informant: "You never can tell whether your partner loves you or not. A man cannot be sure of a woman, and neither the woman of a man. Even if the other says she loves you, you still do not believe it."

One comforting conclusion can be drawn. The Kapsiki realize that the relationship between the sexes is not as they would ideally like to have it. They believe that people should be able to depend on each other, but the difference between the ideal and reality is far too great for them to retain any illusions.

Among the Mandara tribes the Kapsiki marriage system is more or less modal. From some small groups north of the Kapsiki similar situations have been found (Richards 1977). For the larger groups like Mofu and Mafa (see map) marriage seems somewhat more stable. Comparison is not easy as reports do not habitually give comparable data on marriage duration (Vaughan 1964).

The systematization of secondary marriages is typical Kapsiki. Rules and regulations for marriages vary considerably between the mountain tribes. Important in this respect is the relationship between the intervillage fighting and the *zamale* — enmity. Women run from enemy to enemy.

On an African scale, the most astonishing fact is that very unstable marriages occur in a patrilineal virilocal society. African ethnography has given many, now classic, examples of matrilineal groups with high instability versus stable marriages in patrilineal groups. Thus, marital instability tends to be associated with matrilineality not patrilineality. The marriage system of matrilineal tribes is very different, however, even where the stability is about the same. As all Mandara tribes are patrilineal, the whole area forms a notable exception. Some factors for this marital instability have been mentioned. As a small-scale society continually assaulted for slaves by a stronger enemy, lacking central authority or coherent organization about the village level, often at war among themselves, Kapsiki society is quite fragmented. The local patrilineages never had a strong hold on members nor, consequently, on women. This fragmentation made it easy for women to leave their husbands, thus increasing tensions and strife between the villages. The strong economic position of the women bolstered by the introduction of peanut cultivation contrasts with the relative weakness of her ties with the local groups and with her children. Finally, infant and child mortality are exceptionally high, inducing women to move on to improve their fortune and inducing men to try desperately to gain more of that scarce commodity: people.

6

The Walls of the Compound

In the preceding chapters we have explored the relevant social groups making up Kapsiki society and have dwelt extensively on the marriage system which has serious repercussions on the life of the individual. In this chapter we shall explore what values guide Kapsiki life and how the Kapsiki individual copes with his or her social environment. Starting with the dominant values on the lowest level of social integration, the individual, we shall see how Kapsiki life is fraught with a number of conflicting claims leading up to a precarious balance for each individual's existence. Throughout, the tensions inherent in the marriage system make themselves felt at each and every level of social life.

Privacy and Self-sufficiency

The one important value associated with the individual is the sense of privacy throughout Kapsiki culture. A *rhE* is the habitat of a *za* (man) who, together with the women he has in his home at the moment, with his children and occasionally with his brother, forms the main social unit in the fabric of everyday life. In fact the village, as we have seen, consists of a more or less loose agglomerate of individual men who relate to each other by kinship, affinity and friendship but never give up their fundamental autonomy.

The ideal type of a *za*, master of the home, is a mature man, well-to-do, who is as careful as he is adroit in conducting his social relations and in balancing his rights and obligations to protect his cherished autonomy and invaluable privacy. He never bothers other men and they in return are careful not to be a nuisance to him. A *za* performs his sacrifices according to divination to prevent the supernatural world from intruding. His granaries should be well-filled, his huts full of people. Women are attracted by his wealth and stay in his compound bearing his children and working on his fields. He should be generous with his wealth, give frequent beer parties and furnish his many friends with a small gift of kola nuts, tobacco or beer. His friends may reside in the same village, but at least one of them should belong to an enemy village to which he has made himself a ritual ally. A "big man," as the Kapsiki would say, is a valiant fighter on the battlefield, a successful hunter and an indefatigable cultivator.

Thus self-sufficiency, circumspection and privacy are the most important Kapsiki values. As we saw, the compound wall effectively shields the compound in-group from the out-group. Visitors feel free to enter the forecourt, but hesitate to pass the entrance pillars of the stone wall. Calling *"mbeli ki rhE?"* (anybody home?) they wait for an answer, an invitation to enter. Inside the compound the personal huts are always locked; among the very first items of European material culture the Kapsiki have adopted, the locks secure personal privacy. The amount of thefts in no way justifies this security-mindedness, and the many practical and ritual precautions against thieves stem from this norm that no one should be allowed or even tempted to interfere with someone else's business. The same holds for the relations of the man vis-a-vis other men. What a neighbor of kinsmen does, says or thinks is his proper right. Whether he marries a new wife, beats his old one, performs sacrifices or quarrels with strangers is up to him. One should stay clear of that, as interference with someone else implies making his business and his problems one's own!

In many traditional stories this norm is exemplified. In one of them someone has boasted that he could devour a whole bull. This should be proven, so the headman summons him to put his money where his mouth is. Panicked, he consults a blacksmith, a clever man like all blacksmiths. Following his advice he had the bull slaughtered and cooked the next morning. Of course many people gather in his compound to cook, see and perhaps to eat. He has the portions of meat set out in his forecourt and then starts eating. Nibbling small bites from each of the portions he dashes to and fro never finishing one part. At last one of the spectators cannot hold his tongue: "You should finish one portion and then proceed with the next one." Expecting just this, the eater immediately retorts: "If you know so much eat it yourself." The onlookers castigate the quick-tongued spectator: "Yes, you should eat it yourself, so finish the whole bull on your own." This second man makes a courageous attempt at it but inevitably fails and is punished. The first one is saved.

This non-interference and self-sufficiency permeates social and political relations. A Kapsiki does not suffer himself to be forced, neither by his kinsmen, nor by the village chief. He knows who to ask for advice, behaves circumspectly but has the sole responsibility for his own affairs. Comments from lineage elders, ward or village chiefs never exceed the level of advice, although it may be backed up by the respect one has for the officeholder.

Privacy prevails in various transactions. Three types of transactions are fully private in Kapsiki life. They are the asking of loans, brideprice negotiations and sacrifices. These three represent the three spheres in which a man should contain his self-sufficiency: his relations with other men, his relations with his wives and affines, and his relationship to *shala*, his god. Against other men one should be attentive as no one else will champion one's cause. Versus in-laws one has to be respectful but cautious, not trusting them too much, always bringing in witnesses for any payment. *Shala* should be held at arm's length; sacrifices aim at keeping him out of the house more than at a harmonious relationship.

A real *za* should not be afraid to stand for his rights, even to fight for them and to react quickly on any offense given. Thus the Kapsiki have gained the reputation of being quarrelsome (Smith 1969:36) and difficult to rule. Some other values tie in with this autonomous though circumspect way of behaving. An important way of balancing social obligations is by means of *ntsehwele,* trickery, cunning. *Ntsehwele* is a personal quality (van Beek 1982:195). People having it can manipulate others, trick them and have them act against their own good. One traditional story may illustrate that *ntsehwele* is the way to achieve one's end, by trickery if possible. It illustrates too that this personal quality is considered as a cumulative entity, to be added upon by *ntsehwele* from other people:

> A chief had butchered his bull and asked his children: "Who can keep this meat for about a month for me without decay?" Two of them showed up, saying they would do it. Both took a leg and went home. The first one had explained to the chief that he would use his own *ntsehwele* only, so he put the beef with a lot of leaves into a new jar, sealing in with wax. The second, claiming that he would double his *ntsehwele* with that of someone else, struck up an agreement with a butcher: "This is good beef, and it means a lot to me. Cut it up and sell it as yours, but the day the chief reclaims his part, be sure and give me a similar one." The butcher agreed. The first man spent his days watering the leaves to cool the jar, but the second one rested. About a month later the chief asked for his meat. The second Kapsiki asked the butcher to refund a similar leg of beef, a huge one just like the chief's. When he presented it to the chief, the latter said: "Wonderful, that is the leg I gave you. Surely you have doubled your *ntsehwele* with that of someone else. But where is the first man, who would rely upon his own *ntsehwele* alone?" There he came, carrying his jar. But when he opened it, a swarm of flies struck the chief's

face and penetrating odor filled the forecourt, so the chief had him
killed. The successful competitor explained how he did it: "I am not
alone; I have mixed my *ntsehwele* with that of a friend to make it bigger.
Thus I kept the meat just as fresh as the day it was cut."

More often than not *ntsehwele* is the attribute of people of inferior status,
like blacksmiths. In the traditional stories weak and harmless beings have it,
like donkeys, orphans, lepers, the youngest brother or the youngest wife.
The possessor "par excellence" of *ntsehwele* in these stories is the squirrel.

In daily life, as in the stories, it is by cunning that people with a weak
social position can nevertheless do as they like. The concept of *ntsehwele*
implies a minority situation, in which the possessor of the attribute
constantly faces a fiendish majority. Women, marrying in a large family,
have to be cunning and resourceful to carve out their niche in the
household. Just as in the traditional stories the tricky squirrel again and
again beats the stupid leopard, but never really gets the upper hand, the
cunning blacksmiths can stay clear of the claims that non-smiths lay upon
them, but retain their inferior social position. Women, likewise, try to steer
their own course, free from interference by their husband or in-laws. Very
rich men are not associated with *ntsehwele*. Thus, *ntsehwele* is one of the
means for any Kapsiki to cope with a potentially hostile social environment,
but a mechanism which has to be grounded firmly in a solid material basis.

Relations with Kin

To maintain his place in society a Kapsiki depends on his or her kinsmen.
Two categories may be important for help or advice in daily life: agnatic
and cognatic kinsmen, including the important person of the mother's
brother. Let us consider the agnatic first. In this patrilineal society the
patrilineal kinsmen would be the obvious party to turn to in case of need. In
our overview of the main social units of Kapsiki society in Chapter Three,
we drew a picture of clans and lineages as a skeleton of social life which has
to be fleshed out with the relationships between kinsmen and the impact of
clan and lineage membership upon a person's life.

Clan membership provides social identity within the village. If in an
encounter between two men social identity is relevant, it is their clan
membership that is mentioned as a definition of status. Anybody's clan
membership is well-known by all village people. This circumscript function
of clans clearly shows at the high times of the year, in the festivities, burials,
harvest rituals and wars. The same holds for the lineages: social identity,
ceremonial positions and group stereotypes follow lineage membership.
Still, these larger institutionalized patrigroups bear few corporate

characteristics, so their role in everyday social life is small.

Far more important in this respect are immediately patrilineal kin, as mentioned in Chapter Three, descending from a recent ancestor, say FaFaFa, and making up what might be called a sublineage. This group bears no proper name nor title, but it does form a kind of corporate group controlling property and settling debts. One frequently encounters these agnatic kinsmen through the custom of building compounds near a FaBr or FaFaBrSo. They are consulted on all kinds of important decisions such as marriage preparations, and this group is invited to drink the sacrificial beer. A lineage sacrifice called *melE keshi* (sacrifice of the ancestor) reunites these kinsmen and their progeny.

One major incentive for the cooperation of immediate patrilineal kin is their shared interest in their father's or grandfather's property. They have some claims on one another's goods. Land rights may provide an example. In principle all property is private and individual property. Fields thus belong to the man who has claimed and cultivated them for the first time. Nowadays, however, all cultivable land has been claimed for more than two generations, so all fields have gone through a process of inheritance:

About two generations ago *Talema* opened up a field of about one and a half hectares. He supported his claim by sinking in long stones every 30 meters along the border. After a long and fruitful cultivation he divided this field between his three sons, *Zera Canzha, Deli NewakE* and *Teri McE,* marking the division with small stones every 10 meters. These men, all dead by now, divided their parts between their respective sons, marking the fields with small earth and grass ridges.

The present situation can be mapped thus:

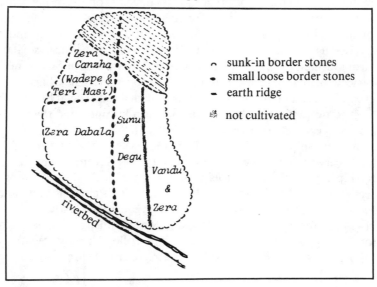

The genealogy is as follows:

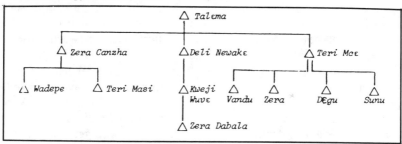

The genealogy in the above-mentioned case in fact shows a sublineage. Although the group does not control the whole field as one body, they have their vested interests in the property of their brethren, as they are each other's potential heirs. If one of them should die, the other brothers would inherit his wives, cultivate his fields, take his cattle or other wealth and, more reluctantly, pay his debts.

If *Vandu,* son of *Teri McE* were to die, his son would inherit his fields, and none of the other kinsmen would be involved. However, should *Zera Dabala* die childless (a small chance as he has fathered two living and healthy pairs of twins!) his fields would be claimed by the other descendants of *TalEma,* probably by *Wadepe,* the eldest one.

Any estate should be divided by the sons of the deceased father, the oldest son serving as trustee. His is the responsibility for the division of property, although quite often he will keep all movables:

> The property of *Vandu Ntsu,* an important man in the village as he has fathered scores of children, is kept by *Rhampa,* the eldest of his numerous offspring. *Vandu's* wife also settled at *Rhampa's.* She stayed with her much older husband to the end, and he had promised her that she could keep all the clothes and money herself. So after his death she took all her belongings with her to *Rhampa's* compound, thus backing up *Rhampa's* claim to the estate. *Vandu* had said before his death that his daughter *Rebecca* should divide his possessions among her brothers. This was quite an exceptional arrangement because *Rebecca,* who as a daughter had no claim at stake, was rich herself and was married to an important and wealthy man; she could therefore be expected to divide evenly and rightly.

If the old man had lived with one of several sons, this son—often the youngest—would have inherited the compound. In the majority of cases inheritance gives no problems whatsoever, as the total estate to be inherited does not often represent much of a sum and because the number of potential heirs is limited. Kapsiki society is at best a static society demographically, and so a man usually does not have many sons. Most inheritance cases (*zemerhE* or eat the compound) occur between father and son without any brothers being involved.

One cultural mechanism further restricts the number of heirs: for most important valuables (cattle, land, money, clothes) heirs have already been appointed long before death. A Kapsiki *za* decides for himself who is to get his riches, as is befitting for a truly autocratic individual. In his *midimte,* literally "speak about death," he states who is going to get what. Walking through the fields with his son, he points out the cattle that are his and he says which beasts are to be his son's. He gives the names of the people tending his flocks and of the Fulani friends with whom he has been keeping his wealth, so a son can reclaim his father's possessions after his death. The fact that a father has to teach the boy which property is his is highly relevant, and illustrates the high level of privacy permeating Kapsiki culture. The total amount and whereabouts of a man's property is known only to him, and he has to instruct his son in this knowledge lest the movables be lost, especially the cattle. Friends, neighbors or kinsmen may be the witnesses of the often casually posed *midimte,* withholding any comment or critical reaction. After the man's death they see to its fulfillment. If people do not follow this "last" will, the deceased is expected to haunt them in the form of leprosy or of a big snake, and the estate will whither away within a year.

A *midimte* is the more important if there are no children to inherit. In this case a man may choose between his brothers. Usually the preference is for full brothers, or as the Kapsiki say, brothers of the same mother, but this is not a hard and fast rule. In the above-mentioned land case *DEgu* has stated once that in case of his death *Sunu,* his full brother, will take his portion only after *Vandu,* his half-brother, has agreed.

Inheritance only poses problems when valuable property has to be divided, especially cattle, money and claims on creditors, and in those instances the absence of a *midimte* gives rise to serious conflicts within the sublineage:

> *Deli Kweji,* from the *maze* clan, died young leaving a young widow and a boy of about 11 years behind. He was rich, owning more than 20 head of cattle. The very night of the elaborate burial people began to whisper accusations. All kinds of rumors about his wealth circulated in the village mentioning scores of so-called *midimte. Deli* had his cattle herded by Fulani friends, and nobody knew exactly where and how many. Only the boy happened to know more about it (of course the Mororo Fulani knew it too, but not one of them will ever divulge anything about the cattle they guard). *Deli's* half-brothers put considerable pressure on the

boy to say what he knew about these beasts. As the boy was still too small to own such capital one of the brothers, in this case *Tshimeha Maze,* was to play guardian over him and his property. The next day the village was plagued by rumors about black magic. *Tshimeha* was supposed to have killed *Deli* by magic, and even the heavy oath *Tshimeha* performed on his dead brother's body did not convince many outsiders because the interest at stake was too big. The boy had mentioned 100.000 CFA ($400.00) that was hidden somewhere.

When *Tshimeha* was seen three months later in new clothes riding a new horse, most people were convinced that the boy would never see his father's money. A year later *Deli's* widow married *KwafashE,* another brother of *Deli* and the boy went to live with them.

So brothers, full as well as classificatory, hide their wealth from each other. The cattle they own are herded by non-kin, pastoral Fulani friends. Practically no one tends his own cattle. The reason for this, they state, is to evade paying with their beasts for the debts of their brethren. Formerly, when manslaughter had to be paid, all kinsmen were taxed and cattle were taken away by the claimant's party if they could find any or knew of any. The only way of safeguarding one's possessions against the transgressions of brothers is to tuck them away.

Smaller debts made by a member of a lineage or sublineage can be claimed from agnatic kinsmen too. Thus, the debts of a deceased brother have to be repaid by his heirs. Land may be a sensitive issue in this because the lineages do not want to lose their claims on fields, and they heavily resent any land sale a less upright brother may contract:

> *Kweji Da* was still waiting for two goats his son-in-law (same clan, different lineage) owed him for *Kweji's* fertile daughter. In compensation he obtained the right to cultivate a field of a lineage member of his son-in-law for several years. A young lineage brother, *Sunu Kwadaheru,* wanted to use that field, paid the two goats and cultivated the field. On hearing this, his older lineage brother *LEwa* refunded him the goats, saying it was up to the older members of the lineage to pay the debts. The same *Kweji Da* sold some fields to *Deli KwayEngu* (different clan). Having no children and many fields, *Kweji* was more interested in the money he received for it than in ensuring the usufruct for his lineage brothers' progeny. The other clan members were livid, and a rich one among them refunded *Kweji Da* and from that time "commanded" the field.

Lineage members may cultivate each other's fields without any compensation or counterclaim. "One cannot prohibit a brother," the

Kapsiki state, and the main reason is that the lineage or sublineage has no sanctions against its members. Even when one of them sells the property the others are entitled to inherit, they cannot do anything except to get very angry and refund the money to the buyer, lest they lose their rights. No action is taken against the anti-social clansman since one cannot prosecute a brother. Loans are never given to a brother as one has no way of enforcing repayment. Powerless against the self-willed kinsman, one can only "sit tight, look with the eyes," and pay. The autonomy of the individual dominates the relations within the agnatic group too. Thus, full brothers, being competitors for eventual wealth and responsible for each other's foolishness and greed, are often at odds. Nevertheless, brothers should be close and conflict between them is an infraction of the ideal state of affairs. The behavioral standard is thus generally at odds with reality, a conflict built into the structure of Kapsiki society, in which the social norm of privacy and self-sufficiency is dominant. Many Kapsiki stories are about siblings and they are almost always antagonistic: they compete for women and in some stories even castrate each other! As stories go, the younger brother always wins. Another favorite expression of suppressed hostility—accusations of witchcraft and sorcery—follows the same lines. Although the Kapsiki should by no means be viewed as a witch-ridden society, hints and rumors of sorcery circulate within the lineage. Witchcraft accusations, if they are voiced, often occur between wives of brothers. Despite these tendencies the Kapsiki still try to uphold the ideal; brothers should be best friends and anyone without brothers is truly bereft. When an understanding of our European society dawned upon my informants, they pitied me for "having no brothers."

There are, of course, other kinsmen. Two crucial relatives for any Kapsiki are his father and his mother's brother. The first one is obviously the closest patrilineal authority, but the *kwesegwe* (MoBr) is also of great importance, as we saw already in the marriage proceedings. His authority is indisputedly strong and far-reaching. "The *kwesegwe* is more *yita* (father) than the father himself," the Kapsiki say. His nephew may address him as "father" to express his respect, and any Kapsiki father behaves quite circumspectly vis-a-vis his wife's brother. The *kwesegwe* indeed has a number of strongholds: he represents the family that gave its daughter in marriage and a fertile woman is never wholly paid for. Any father is therefore in the debt of his in-law. Being mother's closest kin, the *kwesegwe* wields a supernatural sanction in his ability to curse his sister's son. Aside from the mother's curse, which is strongest of all but rarely occurs, the curse of a *kwesegwe* is most feared as it can bring about illness, sterility and death. No formal utterance is needed. An uncle just has to think "bad thoughts" about his nephew and the *bedla* (curse) is there. The *kwesegwe* may even be unaware of it. In divination misfortune is often adduced to such a curse. The *kwesegwe* who can invoke the curse can lift it too. A special ritual, in which he spits beer over the afflicted kinsman, takes care of that.

The actual cursing of a nephew goes against the Kapsiki grain. The uncle, who holds great authority over his nephew at times of ritual and ceremony, is in the daily walk of life very well-disposed towards him. The norm is that he should really love his sister's son and quite often this norm is well-met. "Without a *kwesegwe* you have no one who loves you," the Kapsiki say. One's mother is a loving relative and so should be her brother. In an affectionate mood the uncle is called "mother" and he should protect and guide his nephew, and help him with his brideprice, just as he should counsel and help his niece. The sister's son has some well-defined privileges in his uncle's compound; he can take small items on a whim, a piece of string for example or some meat from a newly slaughtered goat and no *kwesegwe* will ever be angry about it. The nephew should help his mother's brother in weeding a new field, in building or roofing a new hut and should assist in all kinds of chores when his people are ill. He has a very special prerogative: he should slaughter any of his uncle's goats and, the last service of all, he digs his uncle's grave. Still, when inside his uncle's compound the sister's son behaves quite circumspectly. Singing and wailing are out; body noises are to be suppressed and never is he to wash his hands in the hollowed stone where the goats are watered lest all the goats die!

On the other hand, the authority of the father, although well-marked, is far more formal and easygoing. His is the everyday authority. An adult son has an easy and intimate relationship with his father, each respecting the other in an affective balance. The Kapsiki explain the difference between father and uncle in economic terms. The father, they say, has invested in his children through his brideprice. The child is his gain and his goal, so a good relation with it is a means of maximizing his gain. The *kwesegwe* finds his gain through the fertile marriage of his sister; thanks to her marriage he receives a substantial amount of wealth and thanks to her offspring he can keep it. His interest is more in keeping the relationship intact rather than in the actual person of his kinsman.

The importance of the mother's kinsmen shows in the constitution of the only kind of kin group outside agnatic lineage and family. It is called the *hwelefwe,* meaning "seed" or "offspring." It is a circle of relatives around a person making up a group with unclear boundaries; the core of the *hwelefwe* consists of one's matrilineal relatives plus the descendants of male members of that matrilineage (van Beek 1978:77). No property, title or name is attached to a *hwelefwe,* but in the traditional situation of warring villages its importance should not be underestimated. Matrilineal relatives usually live a long way off, in other villages throughout the Kapsiki territory. Whoever travels abroad uses these relations extensively. Hospitality and protection in any strange village are offered by members of one's *hwelefwe,* and formerly all commerce followed the lines of matrilineal kinship. For women these ties are of utmost importance. Women form the mobile element in society, as they go to other markets, visit sisters and daughters off in strange and hostile villages and, of course, as they go from one husband to another. Wherever they go, they look for their *hwelefwe* first in order to be introduced into the village through them. Thus, the mother's brother who is the principal member of this group, is often crucial in the woman's choice of a new spouse. Women visit their matrilineal relatives far more than men and are more involved emotionally with matrilineal kin than with their patrilineal descendants. A Kapsiki woman stated that "a man has his offspring in his lineage, a woman in her *hwelefwe."* A woman will tend to raise the children of a deceased daughter, whereas the orphans of her son get far less attention. Once we heard an old woman refuse to care for her late son's orphans, saying, "Why should I do it? Since when are they my *hwelefwe?"* A few major occasions bring the *hwelefwe* together. This happens in occasional twin festivals and one far more frequent occasion, in burial. In all burials the *hwelefwe* of the deceased gather to dance in honor of the dead relative, accentuating their relationship with the deceased by special dress and ornaments. After the burial rites they have a joint meal and a small communal farewell rite.

Friendship

Life, even in the traditional Kapsiki setting, is more than the total nexus of kinship obligations. The warp of inevitable kinship ties is cross-cut by the woof of informal, chosen relations of one individual with another; i.e., friendship. One has, on the one hand, kinsmen and in-laws, and, on the other, one's friends. These categories seldom overlap. Friendship in Kapsiki society crosses boundaries that the formal structures of the society impose. Friends are often people from other clans and phratries; friendship extends across the castelike barrier of non-smith vs. blacksmith, and may even cross ethnic boundaries. Friendship of a Kapsiki with a pastoral Mbororo Fulani is quite normal.

Friends are important in the easy, informal times of social life. A man often visits his friend's compound to chat or to drink a little beer if his wife has brewed some. Together they walk the village paths, greeting other strollers, exchanging a few puns with a passing woman or perhaps taking a few strands of rope from a mother's brother's compound. The two of them dress up for market and assist in drinking down any beer given to them, in selling the tidbits of their commerce or in pleading with a woman to marry one of them. Problems of the household can in fact only be confided to a friend, and in conflicts with other Kapsiki it is the friend that one runs to first of all. If leisure time is ample they play games with *tserhwe* (beans), and in their evening stroll after the main meal they play or watch *caca*, the officially forbidden game of chance, in someone else's compound. Small gifts such as kola nuts, tobacco or a calabash of beer cement the relationship, although the real test is an economic one; a real friend helps out in financial trouble. At marriage a friend gives beer, sorghum and goats, thus helping in brideprice payment as well as marriage expenses, and he loans his friend considerable sums to pay his debts.

A woman often joins her friend in cutting firewood, fetching water and any other outdoor task. Women tend each others' babies, and they help in plaiting sacs or in selling peanuts on the market. After brewing, small gifts of beer find their way to the friend's hut. If their daughters marry they are inseparable for days, working together at the many kinds of ceremonial food needed for the festivities.

Cross-sex friendship occurs, but not too frequently. With marriage as brittle as it is in Kapsiki society, a friendship between a man and a woman easily turns into a new marriage, so suspicion is always there. Such friendships are restricted to one's own village. A man may be friends with a woman he may not marry, like a close kinswoman forbidden to him by exogamy rules, with a blacksmith's wife outside his endogamy circle, or with his best friend's wife whom he has no intention of marrying, lest he spoil a good friendship.

Men generally have a more widely dispersed network of friendship ties than women. Mens' friends are scattered throughout the village and over other villages. A woman's best friend is often a next-door neighbor, the Kapsiki women being much less mobile inside the village than their high mobility between villages would suggest. When first joining her husband a young wife stays close to the *rhE* and just joins a few neighbors. She often feels quite alone and rejected: "All men are against me; are they not men? But all women are against me too, as their husbands do not love them because of me," a clan brother's wife once complained. When they are older and more established in the village, women gradually regain the freedom of movement they had before marriage and their friends may be farther away. However, just like very old men, they eventually become quite isolated and lonely, and feelings of self-pity and self-denigration abound:

> (an old woman) "Why should I have a friend? Am I worth a friend? What can I give to her? Neither do I have enemies, as I am not worth it."
> (an old man): "I am too old. Nobody loves me. I cannot prepare *zhazha* (beans mixed with sorghum, often eaten between friends) with a friend. If someone gives me a wife, he is my friend, but who will? No woman-friend do I have. Why should a woman be my friend? Nobody loves me, and people have put magic around my compound, but God protects me. Why?"

Among the friends one may have, one is singled out as a special friend, the *mcE kwatla pela,* the friend who cuts your fingernails (which is done with the big two-edged Kapsiki knives, and indeed does take some trust). Such a friendship has its own ceremonial. One man has his nephew kill one of his goats, brews beer and invites his friend for a full day of feasting, eating and drinking from sunrise until well after sunset, sending his friend home staggering under gifts of beer and meat. About a month later the friend reciprocates. Just after the ceremonies of their *makwa* wedding young women do the same thing, each bride feasting the other on two consecutive days.

Sometimes friends have their children marry each other, but most friends do not want to risk their friendship on an in-law relation. Instead, they prefer to be the "second father" of the friend's newly marrying daughter, or to perform as "initiation father" to the friend's initiate son. This fits in perfectly with the relationships between friends.

Dispute Settlement

An individual Kapsiki strongly resents all interference in his private affairs. Of course he is dependent upon his village and its chief, dependent upon his lineage for land, upon his friends and kinsmen for providing labor in communal working parties, and he easily accepts these kinds of ties. But no chief or official should prescribe or proscribe his way of life, his dealings with other men, his relationship with the supernatural world. If the government wants to do away with gambling and instructs chiefs and ward headmen to put the order into effect, they are in for trouble. Politeness and respect make listeners but not followers. After listening to the advice, counsels and admonitions of the chief, any Kapsiki who happens to be present emphatically states his approval with all measures, and afterwards wanders off on his own without bothering any more about what was said. One could say a conflict between authority and autarchy is inherent in Kapsiki society. In fact, a Kapsiki is for most of his daily life and for the majority of his problems dependent only on himself.

A man or woman can run into trouble in several ways: transgression of taboo, sorcery, debts, conflicting claims on property, and last of all quarrels and disputes. The village chief, as the representative authority, is in the picture only for the last item on the list. For the rest, any formal mundane authority is out. Taboo problems are solved by divination and sacrifice, and debts are settled by *sekwa*, a ritual means by which debtors will be supernaturally killed if they do not pay. Conflicting claims are solved by a rooster ordeal in Mogodé or Kamalé if the old men of the village do not succeed in arranging the matter:

> *Sekwa,* the debt-settling device, is most illustrative of the way Kapsiki handle their own problems. *Sekwa*, in fact, is a bundle of herbs, prepared according to a definite and publicly known recipe, on which roosters are sacrified each year to keep it "working." It works in practice as a threat.

If a debtor, after many reminders and urgings from the creditor, still refuses to pay his dues, the creditor will threaten to put the *sekwa* in the middle of the debtor's compound. If this happens, the Kapsiki profoundly believe all the inhabitants of the compound will die as if stricken by an epidemic. If there is no debt, the people have nothing to fear, even if they sleep right over the *sekwa*. As they say, "the *sekwa* follows the debt." One of the most important areas of debt is—of course—repayment of brideprice. If a wife has left without having children, the in-laws forfeit their brideprice gains. A father-in-law is never a quick refunder, and if the husband does not believe his wife will return he may have to threaten his father-in-law with *sekwa*. Normally the threat is quite sufficient, but some tight-fisted in-laws have to be persuaded by the actual thing. The creditor takes *sekwa* and walks with the bundle of herbs to the in-laws' house, pauses at the doorstep and waits for the money.

Although *sekwa* is considered to be a killer, it is not considered bad manners to resort to it, because there is no other effective means to settle debts. Neither the chief, nor anyone else would be able to encroach on someone's privacy so far as to settle a question as private as debt.

Today the Cameroonian and Nigerian governments are trying to do away with this kind of settlement, and try to centralize all law enforcement in courts held by district chiefs appointed by the government. In Mogodé the *chef de canton,* holding court in the traditional Fulani fashion (although he is himself a Kapsiki), forbids the manufacture and use of *sekwa* ("because it is murder"); as a result he judges a growing number of "divorce" cases himself. In fact, he finances his whole court mainly from the revenues of these cases.

In all these instances the village chief is not involved. His leeway in settling disputes is small and may be best illustrated by an incident at Mogodé market:

At market a woman from Mogodé quarreled with *Kweda* a man from Kamalé just across the Nigerian border. *Kweda* gave her some money more than a year ago. The woman, *KwayEngu,* accepted the gift but did not show up at his compound to marry him. When questioned, she stated that she did not want to go in the first place. *Kweda* reclaimed his six shillings, but *KwayEngu* disputed the amount. She claimed that she had received only four shillings. Big quarrel. The chief moved into the melèe, saying, "It is not right to quarrel in the market. Let us go and sit over there under that tree and discuss the matter." With considerable effort he managed to isolate the man and woman from the crowd of spectators, and spent an hour reconstructing in great detail when, where and under what circumstances the money had been given, even inspecting the stone upon which the coins were placed. At long last the woman gave in and paid the six shillings to her former marriage candidate through the chief.

A small amount of money as in the above case, does not call for drastic measures with *sekwa*, but the chief moved in mainly because of the people in the market, a public place where a very fragile peace prevails. Anyway, debts between a man and woman never are settled by supernatural means, only by discussion and—above all—perseverance.

Chiefs and headman often publicly complain about the unwillingness of their compatriots, who just do as they like regardless of the dire consequences to general well-being. Their complaints find general support:

> After the burial of a blacksmith woman, at a beer party, considerable discussion centered on those people who had ignored the chief's admonitions and had tilled their fields during the funeral dances (a smith burial is double dangerous and the normal restriction on cultivation should be respected even more). One leader of the small Christian community stated, "Those who were first to till their fields speak up first here too (to deny it!). To whom are we speaking here? In our compound many roosters live, but one of them we chose as our *ngulu rhE* (cock-of-the-house, a symbol for the whole household). Likewise we choose the chief. Is he too small? Did we not choose him? We Christians are with you. We respect the chief and tell other people to do so. You have to beg God in the way of our ancestors to take away all these deaths from the village."

Traditional stories and personal histories of old men and women indicate that this clash between individual autarchy and authority is not a new development but was endemic in Kapsiki society long before colonization. With great gusto old men tell how they followed their own will against common consent and the expert opinions of the chief and the elders, but even with current government efforts to centralize authority, a trend towards greater autarchy is discernible. Nowadays people do not need the protection of the village against slave raiding, and the villages gradually disperse over the plateau and the valleys, loosening ties and diminishing responsibilities.

An early investigator of the Kapsiki noted his impression that Kapsiki society "suffit à elle-même," was itself enough: a self-reliant people which needed no one else and resented intrusion from outside (Podlewski 1966). This still holds today both for the whole society and for the individual Kapsiki. Self-reliance, autonomy and individual assertiveness are basic attitudes for women and men; in conflict resolution, in decision-making and in marriage relations people are on their own. This should not be viewed as a sign of disintegration of a former communally oriented society, but as a result of historical processes bearing upon a marginal area (van Beek 1986a). Compared to other African tribes, this Mandara situation is not standard. West and Central African societies usually are much more communally oriented and less individualistic than the Kapsiki. In this respect the Mandara tribes show, one might say, some western traits. How this may enhance modernization will be explored in the last chapter.

7

Kapsiki and the Outside World

Kapsiki society is changing. The loose conglomeration of autonomous villages gradually is becoming a part of either the Cameroonian or the Nigerian national state. The first sporadic contacts with the colonial administrators did not succeed in opening up the relatively isolated mountain area before World War II. The building of a road from Mokolo to Garoua, just before World War II, running straight through the centre of Kapsiki territory, changed matters. From the Nigerian side a road brought all traffic to Kamalé, at the foot of the plateau which is largely in the Cameroons. The last wars between the villages were fought in the 1950's, but the two preceding decades had already seen a gradual decrease in intervillage fighting. The Kapsiki feel very positive about the colonial pacification of the area. Although peace means loss of an arena in which to show off one's bravery, it intensified contact between villages. One of the main consequences has been the organization of markets. In pre-colonial times the Kapsiki knew no regular markets, commerce being restricted to individual traders commuting between tribes and villages, relying on individual friendships for safety and hospitality. Markets brought European goods along: clothes, finery, shoes, utensils and implements, later to be supplemented by torches, oil lamps and now transistor radios, which were still an exception in the 1970's. Clothing has changed drastically in the last twenty years. Traditional women's gear, a simple "cache sexe" of leather or some leaves, is forbidden in independent Cameroon, although it is still worn in the remote villages in Nigeria. Men no longer content themselves with an oiled goatskin, but feel naked without a "boubou," the Fulani-style loose-hanging gown adopted throughout North

154

Cameroon. Only on ritual occasions, at a sacrifice or a burial, do they wear their ancestor's goatskin loin clothes without a boubou.

Trading with the outside world has been two-sided, as the Kapsiki sell peanuts. Supplanting the traditional cultivation of indigenous groundnuts by the women, the cultivation of this cash crop fell within their sphere and its cash income enhances the old Kapsiki system of female independence and mobility. The introduction of cash crops, as we have stated, has increased female autonomy and probably heightened marriage instability.

Tourism has been another influence. The last two decades have marked an increase in this kind of European contact with Kapsikiland. A hotel was built in Rhoumsiki attracting tourists from all western countries and even from the Cameroonian South to admire the strange and beautiful landscape. The intensive tourism in the Kapsiki area has had surprisingly superficial effects on the Kapsiki themselves. Many tourists "doing" the area are appalled by the scores of small kids asking for a "cadeau" whenever a tourist bus passes by. No one in Rhoumsiki ever poses for a picture without asking for money. However, the effect is mainly on the young boys who linger around the hotel precincts posing as guides, trying to sell a few Kapsiki bronze pipes or bracelets, hoping for a good tip and— above all—dreaming of a gentle pair of tourists who will take them to Europe. A few village boys have indeed been taken to Europe by gentle-but-not-so-wise-tourists. Although the trips in many ways proved to be disasters, miraculous tales fill the eager ears of many a wistful child.

With the opening of the area, new religions came too. Most missions established themselves in Kapsikiland after World War II and on the whole have met only with limited success. Only in Baza, Nigeria, has the Roman Catholic mission been able to build up a considerable congregation.

Whereas the relationship with Christianity is limited in scale as well as in time, the Kapsiki and Higi have had centuries of contact with Islam, or at least with Islamic warriors. From early in the sixteenth century, the Mandara hills have been scorched by Muslim slave raiders and on the whole most mountain people have effectively resisted both slave raids and Islam. Since independence and pacification, however, Islam has made considerable inroads into the Kapsiki and Higi society. Integration into the larger society for present-day Kapsiki implies assimilation with Muslim Fulani culture, with a "Fulanised" North Cameroon. For those who want to become merchants, who need contacts outside the tribal domain and respect from other tribesmen and townspeople, Islam is the easiest way to gain all this. Should one aspire to trade on a larger scale, a pilgrimage to Mecca furnishes the desired and respected *el hadj* title, which opens still more doors. The progress of Islam, however, is limited to its own channels. Beyond the ambitions of political functionaries and merchants there is little reason to change religion, and, although not fiercely loyal to their cultural heritage, the Kapsiki tend not to change without a clear and substantial reason.

The combined impact of nationalism, missions and tourism have, however, begun to bring about a sense of tribal identity where it never existed before. Throughout, we have described the Kapsiki as a loose conglomerate of separate villages and that is just what they always have been and to a large extent still are. They never formerly called themselves by one tribal name. Kapsiki means "they who germinate the millet," a part of the beer-making process, which in fact is only characteristic for four villages; Higi is the name by which their Marghi neighbors called them *(hegi* means locust). Since colonization, the whole cluster area is indicated with one name. Contact between villages is building up despite old hostilities, new rivalries and differences in language. Tourists everywhere keep asking for "the Kapsiki." Despite their continuous feelings of inferiority to other cultures, especially to Fulani and European culture, they have developed a sort of tribal unity, or, one could say, a kind of tribal unity is being forced upon them. Pride in their own ancestral ways is practically absent. Young Kapsiki suffer from strong feelings of self-denigration, sensing themselves part of a backward area where the old traditions still hamper new growth and development. Many of them easily give up their sacrifices without becoming either Christian or Muslim, but in

The school children of Mogodé are marched off to the local celebration of independence.

many other respects the traditional system is very tenacious. The women still go from husband to husband, brideprice payments have to be made and repaid, if not in goats then in money, and arguments and fights about women quickly flare up in the afternoon of a market day, when everyone has had his share of beer. The governments of both Cameroon and Nigeria try to strengthen marital ties in polygamous marriages by fining second husbands, but this scarcely keeps the women from moving around. By crossing the international border they put themselves beyond the control of their government, and the enforcement of Cameroonian regulation in Nigeria or vice versa, is still very difficult, despite treaties and consultations between the local authorities. The net result of this government regulation is practically nil.

The border actually preserves the traditional system even though it cuts the Kapsiki and Higi into two separate units. Although the influence on everyday life is very limited, the two areas are gradually separating into two ethnic units, each with its own name and sense of identity. In Cameroon, the Kapsiki are included in one administrative unit (a canton called Mogodé). In Nigeria, the Michika district unites most of the Higi villages. Differences between the two districts began to show from the time of the Biafran war. The Nigerian Higi have quickly descended from their steep and rocky hills and moved out westwards into Marghi territory. Aggressive and capable farmers as they are, they take up modern cultivation techniques and in good years harvest many times the old amounts of sorghum. In Cameroon this option is not open to the Kapsiki because the Mandara mountains extend well beyond the neighboring Mofou and Matakam tribes. In some places along the road many Kapsiki are taking up trade as a supplement to agriculture, and today Mogodé is quickly developing into a regional trading center. The easy accessibility of Nigeria, just downhill from Mogodé, gives the village a very favorable location for trade. In both cases, as everywhere in rural Africa, boys and girls increasingly attend school and enter the larger society. Although by far the majority of Kapsiki boys and girls do not finish their CEP (primary schooling), an increasing number do leave the area in order to obtain secondary education. A few Higi boys from Michika have studied at universities, mainly in Zaria. However, most schooled Kapsiki and Higi return to their fields, to cultivate the stone terraces just as has been done for ages. When a job is found in the "outside" world, they easily assimilate the dominant town culture and may not return.

On the whole, the opening of the area since the 1950's has resulted in a quickly accelerating pace of change. The part of the research carried out in 1972-73 could not have been done in the 1980's. In the whole mountain area people are moving quickly into more modern times without too many problems. In many parts of Africa rapid changes give rise to religious movements, witchcrazes or other indications of social pathology; not so in the Mandara mountains. Perhaps the values these peoples developed as a result of a long history of marginality will enable them to take the inevitable changes in stride.

Preparing for the future.

Author's Notes

1) At the end of the 1970's a marked inflation in brideprices has set in, doubling or even tripling the *wume*. One of the reasons for this is the fast growing number of Kapsiki who enter administrative positions; they not only are able to pay substantive sums, but also cannot be expected to labor in the fields or to pay when children are born. The total value of these additional gifts has to be calculated in the lump sum. Anyway this tendency towards "selling" daughters is gradually becoming an accepted, although not appreciated, custom.

2) We have used Barnes' demographical method in calculating the mean marriage expectation (Barnes 1949:1967). A 10% sample of each compound had been interrogated regarding their marital history, using the Kapsiki definition of a marriage as a guideline. Running away to a new husband implies the severing of the old tie, *de facto* divorce. Return to the former husband has not been counted as a new marriage, but as the continuation of the old one, thus conforming to the indigenous definition of the situation. The answers to our questioning proved to be quite reliable; for a number of marriages we received information from both spouses independently, and both sources conformed sufficiently to warrant a high general level of validity. The total number of interviews was 55 men and 88 women with a grand total of 820 extant and past marriages.

Literature Cited

Baker, R.L. & Zubeiro, Y. 1955. The Higis of Bazza Clan. *Nigeria* 47:213-222.

Barnes, J.A. 1949. Measures of divorce frequency in simple societies. *Journal of the Royal Anthropological Institute* 79:37-62.

Barth, H. *Reisen und Entdeckungen in Nord und Central Afrika in den Jahren 1849-1855* 5 Vols. Gotha.

van Beek, W.E.A. 1975. The religion of everyday life: an investigation into the concepts of religion and magic, *Explorations in the Anthropology of Religion; essays in honor of J. Van Baal,* W.E.A. van Beek and J.H. Scherer (eds.), Leiden VKI 74:55-70.

_____. 1977. Color terms in Kapsiki, *Papers in Chadic Linguistics,* P. Newman & R. Ma (eds.), Leiden, pp. 13-20.

_____. 1978. *Bierbrouwers in de bergen; de Kapsiki en Higi van Noord-Kameroen* Mededelingen van het Instituut voor Culturele Antropologie te Utrecht bi, 12,

_____. 1979. Traditional religion as a locus of change, *Official and Popular Religion,* P.H. Vrijhof & J.J. Waardenburg (eds.) pp. 514-543. The Hague, Mouton.

_____. 1981. Eating like a blacksmith: symbols in Kapsiki ethno-zoology *Symbolic Anthropology in the Netherlands.* P.E. de Josselin de Jong & E. Schwimmer (eds.) pp. 114-124, Leiden.

_____. 1982. Les Savoirs Kapsiki, *La Quête du Savoir; essays pour une anthropologie de l'éducation du Cameroun.* R. Santerre & C. Mercier-Tremblay (eds.), pp. 180-207. Presses Univ. Laval

_____. 1982b. Les Kapsiki, in Cl. Tardits *Contribution de la recherche ethnologique à l'historie des civilisations du Cameroun.* Paris, CNRS, 113-119.

_____. 1982c Eating like a blacksmith; symbols in Kapsiki ethnozoology in P.E. de Josselin de Jong & E. Schwimmer (eds.) *Symbolic Anthropology in the Netherlands* VKI 95: 114-125.

_____. 1983. Sacrifice in two African Communities. *Nederlands Tijdschrift voor de Theologie,* 121-131.

_____. 1983. Sacrifice in two African Communities. *Nederlands Tijdschrift voor de Theologie,* 121-131.

_____. 1986a. L'état, ce n'est pas nous, Cultural proletarization in Cameroon in W. van Binsbergen, F. Reyntens & G. Hesseling (eds.) *State and Local Community in Africa.* Antwerp, ARDOC 1986, 2/3/4: 65-88.

_____. 1986b. Kindersterfte en huwe lÿksmobiliteit: de Kapsiki van Noord-Kameroen, in W. Hoogbergen & M. de Theye (eds.) *Vruchtbaar Onderroek: Essays ter ere van Douwe Jongmans.* Utrecht, JCAU 24: 147-165.

_____. 1986c. The ideology of building: the interpretation of compound patterns among the Kapsiki of North Cameroon, in H. Fokkens, P. Benga & M. Bierma (eds.) *Op Zock naar Mens en Materiële Cultuur.* Groningen, BAI: 147-162.

_____. 1987. Identity management in two African Religions in proceedings IAHR-congress, in press.

Cuingnet, M. Les Mada. Bull. de l'IFAN 30, 1062-1139.

David N. 1972. History of Crops and Peoples in North Cameroon to AD 1900. Paper for the Burg Wartenstein Symposium No. 56

Denham, D., Clapperton, H. & Oudnez, B. 1826. *Narrative of Travels and Discoveries in Northern and Central Africa in the Years 1822, 1823 and 1824.* London.

Dominik, H. 1908. *Vom Atlantik zum Tschadese.* Berlin.

Fréchou, H. 1966. *L'élevage et le commerce du bétail dans le Nord-Cameroun.* Mémoires ORSTOM 1966, 13, 2 & 3-125.

Froelich, J.C. 1968. *Les montagnards paleonégritique.* ORSTOM, Cah. Outre Mer 9.

von Graffenried, C. 1984. *Das Jahr des Stieres Ein Opferritual der Zulgo und Gemjek in Nordkamerun.* Freiburg.

Hallaire, A. 1965. *Les Monts du Mandara.* ORSTOM.

Hurault, J. 1958. Quelques aspects de la structure sociale des montagnards Kiridi du Nord-Cameroun, *Bull. de l'IFAN* 20, 1/2: 111-122.

Juillerat, B. 1971. *Les Bases de l'Organisation Sociale chez les Mouktêlê (Nord-Cameroun).* Mém. de l'Institut de l'Ethnologie VIII

Kirk-Greene, A.H.M. 1958. *Adamawa Past and Present.* London, International African Institute.

_____, & Hogbin, A. 1969. *The Emirates of Northern Nigeria.* London.

Lembezat, B. 1961. *Les Populations paiennes du Nord-Cameroun et de l'Adamaoua.* Paris, PUF.

Lukas, R. 1973. *Nicht-Islamische Etnien im Südlichen Tschadraum.* Wiesbaden, Steiner.

_____. 1977. *Die materielle Kultur der nicht islamischen Ethnieen von Nord-Kamerun und Nordostnigeria.* Wiesbaden-Steiner.

Martin, J.-Y. 1970. *Les Matakam du Cameroun.* Paris, Mémoires ORSTOM.

Meek, C.K. 1931. *Tribal Studies in Northern Nigeria.* 2 Vols. London.

Mohrlang, R. 1972. *Higi Phonology.* Studies in Nigerian Languages 2, Zaria.

Le Moigne, J. 1918. Le Pays Conquis du Cameroun du Nord. *Bull. du Comité de l'Afrique Française* 3:94-114, 130-153.

Otterbein, K.F. 1968. Higi armed combat. *Southwestern Journal of Anthropology* 24:195-213.

_____. 1969. Higi Marriage System. *Bull. of the Cult. Res. Inst.* VIII 1, 2.

Podlewski, A.M. 1966. *La Dynamique des Principales Populations du Nord-Cameroun (entre Benoue et Lac Chad)* Cah. ORSTOM Sc. Hum. 3.

Pontié, G. 1973. *Les Guiziga du Cameroun Septentrional.* Mém. ORSTOM 65, Paris.

Richard, M. 1977. *Traditions et Coutumes matrimoniales chez les Mada et les Mouyeng (Nord-Cameroun).* Collection Inst. Anthropos, 10.

Schaller, Y. 1973. *Les Kirdi du Nord Cameroun.* Strassburg.

Seignobos, Ch. 1984. *Nord Cameroun, Montagnes et Hautes Terres.* Rocquevire. Parenthèse.

Smith, D.M. 1969. *The Kapsiki Language.* Ph.D. diss. Michigan State.

Urvoy, Y. 1949. *Histoire de l'Empire du Bornou.* Mémories de l'IFAN.

Vaughan, J.H., Jr. 1964. Religion and the World View of the Marghi. *Ethnology* 3,4: 389-397.

Vincent, J.F. 1971. Divination et possesion chez les Mofu. *Journal Soc. African* Vol. XLI, 2. p. 71-132.

_____. 1972. Données sur le marriage et la situation de la femme Mofu. *Cahiers ORSTOM, Sc.Hum. 9, 3: 309-324.*

_____. 1975. Le chef et la pluie chez les Mofu in Systèmes de Pensée en Afrique Noire I. CNRS, Ivry.

_____. 1976. Conception et déroulement du sacrifice chez les Mofu in Systèmes de Pensée en Afrique Noire II CNRS, Ivry.

_____. 1978. Main gauche, main de l'homme. *Système de Signes,* p. 485-509. Paris, PUF.

_____. 1979. Sur les traces du Major Denham. Cahier d'Étud. Afric., 72, 575-606.

Vossart, J. 1952. Histoire du Sultanat du Mandara. *Et. Camerounaises* 4, 35: 19-52.

BIBL. UNIV. LAUR. UNIV. LIB.

3 0007 00074862 3

DATE DUE - DATE DE RETOUR